THE ART OF WOODWORKING

HAND TOOLS

THE ART OF WOODWORKING

HAND TOOLS

TIME-LIFE BOOKS
ALEXANDRIA, VIRGINIA

ST. REMY PRESS
MONTREAL • NEW YORK

THE ART OF WOODWORKING was produced by
ST. REMY PRESS

PUBLISHER	Kenneth Winchester
PRESIDENT	Pierre Léveillé
Series Editor	Pierre Home-Douglas
Series Art Director	Francine Lemieux
Senior Editors	Marc Cassini (Text)
	Heather Mills (Research)
Art Directors	Normand Boudreault, Luc Germain
	Solange Laberge
Designers	Jean-Guy Doiron, Michel Giguère
Research Editor	Jim McRae
Picture Editor	Christopher Jackson
Writers	Andrew Jones, Rob Lutes
Contributing Illustrators	Ronald Durepos, Jean-Pierre
	Bourgeois, Michel Blais, Jacques
	Perrault, Alain Longpré, Jocelyn
	Veillette, Robert Paquet
Administrator	Natalie Watanabe
Production Manager	Michelle Turbide
System Coordinator	Jean-Luc Roy
Photographer	Robert Chartier

Time-Life Books is a division of Time-Life Inc.,
a wholly owned subsidiary of
THE TIME INC. BOOK COMPANY

TIME-LIFE BOOKS

President	John D. Hall
Vice President	Nancy K. Jones
Editor-in-Chief	Thomas H. Flaherty
Director of Editorial Resources	Elise D. Ritter-Clough
Marketing Director	Regina Hall
Editorial Director	Lee Hassig
Consulting Editor	John R. Sullivan
Production Manager	Marlene Zack

THE CONSULTANTS

Bob Jardinico manages woodworking sales for Colonial Saw Co., a machinery sales and service company based in Kingston, Massachusetts. He also restores antique furniture in his home workshop in Plymouth, Mass.

Giles Miller-Mead taught advanced cabinetmaking at Montreal technical schools for more than ten years. A native of New Zealand, he has worked as a restorer of antique furniture.

Joseph Truini is Senior Editor of *Home Mechanix* magazine. A former Shop and Tools Editor of *Popular Mechanics*, he has worked as a cabinetmaker, home improvement contractor and carpenter.

Hand tools
    p. cm.—(The Art of Woodworking)
Includes index.
ISBN 0-8094-9925-8
1. Woodworking tools
I. Time-Life Books. II. Series
TT186.H36 1993
684' .082—dc20   92-46416
                                CIP

For information about any Time-Life book,
please call 1-800-621-7026, or write:
Reader Information
Time-Life Customer Service
P.O. Box C-32068
Richmond, Virginia
23261-2068

R 10 9 8 7 6 5 4 3 2 1

CONTENTS

Kelly Mehler discusses the
HAND TOOLS EXPERIENCE

I feel fortunate that I was able to get a solid base in hand woodworking during the early part of my career. I got in on the tail end of a traditional cabinetmaking program at an old vocational college run by a master woodworker who had learned his trade in his father's carriage shop. Each student was assigned a bench and a drawer containing the basic hand tools: a plane, a backsaw, chisels, a small hammer, a square, and a marking gauge. As we worked at the benches, the teacher and his helpers walked around the shop, offering assistance. Although there were some heavy machines in the shop, the predominant atmosphere was one of bench work. Our first task was to make a half-lap joint from a rough piece of poplar using only the tools from our drawer. We started by planing one face flat and from that face squared an edge. Then we marked and planed to the finish thickness, cut the piece in half squarely, and outlined the joint. Next, we sawed and chiseled the joint, all the while checking for square. Once we felt we had a good joint, an instructor would inspect it from all sides for square, flatness, and fit. This exercise demanded intense concentration and it provided the groundwork for my attitude toward woodworking. Attention to detail, a respect for handwork, and the importance of good joinery provided firm cornerstones.

Twenty years later, as a professional furnituremaker, I still find that it is important for me to maintain a balance between handwork and machine work. Being in business sets some of the limits. You may not want money to dictate how you work, but it is a major concern if you are going to work wood for a living. The question of whether a particular process should be accomplished by hand or machine raises a number of questions: Which method is more efficient? Which produces better work—or makes a more valuable finished piece?

I feel that dovetails, for example, can be done best by hand. Even with the new generation of jigs, the extra-fine hand-cut look cannot be achieved with a machine; nor is jigging much faster when there are only a few joints to do. Hand-cut dovetails will also give a piece a much greater investment value. On the other hand, planing a rough board by hand doesn't usually add value. It may be rewarding personally, but hand planing isn't more efficient than using a thickness planer, nor are the results better.

There are many occasions when it is quicker to pick up a hand tool than to set up a machine for a simple operation. I usually cut tenon shoulders with a handsaw and chisel rather than working with a band saw or a table saw. But I taper table legs on the jointer, instead of bandsawing to a line and hand planing the legs smooth. Finding the right balance of hand and power tools is a highly individual matter, balancing the combination of efficiency and value that suits each of us.

The author of numerous articles and two videos, Kelly Mehler builds fine furniture in his shop in Berea, Kentucky.

Curtis Erpelding on
MAKING
HAND TOOLS

I've been making my own hand tools for almost as long as I've been woodworking. A friend once asked me, "Why bother when you can buy factory-made hand tools ready to use?" Why indeed? There is no easy answer.

I could say that making my own tools lets me customize them for special jobs. For example, I've made several wooden planes with the pitch of the blade greater than the standard 45 degrees—the angle at which the front of the edge contacts the wood—in order to work difficult grain without tearout. I've also made molding planes with cutting profiles that are simply not available in a store-bought plane or router bit. Another reason that I make my own tools is for the fit. Anyone who has made a wooden-bodied plane knows that in use it has a different feel from a cast iron or steel plane; this is sometimes a benefit. A handle or plane body can be shaped to conform to the hand, and feel comfortable.

Hand-made tools can be superior to manufactured tools, but many of the planes, chisels, and knives I have made are functionally no different from their mass-produced counterparts. For me, function alone is not enough to explain the extra time and effort involved. Some would say then that making hand tools indicates a romantic nature, an attempt to recapture an earlier era, to mimic a purer form of craftsmanship. While I won't deny a certain romantic bent, what little research I have done into the history of the woodworker's craft has convinced me that few workmen ever made their own tools if they could afford not to. Toolmaking as a separate craft predates the Industrial Revolution. Only for the most off-beat job or only if he plied his trade in some isolated corner would the woodworker presume to duplicate or improve on the product of fellow artisans skilled in the specialized manufacture of tools.

No, in the final analysis I guess that I make my own tools simply because I enjoy making tools. Toolmaking, like furniture making, boat building, or instrument making, is a discipline unto itself. The main difference I suppose is that when I complete a piece of furniture, I send it into the world and it is no longer part of my life. But when I make a tool, it joins my family of other tools. And, after I deliver that piece of furniture I stand back and think with satisfaction, "I made that—and I made it with the tools that I also made."

Curtis Erpelding builds custom furniture in his shop in Port Orchard, Washington.

Toshio Odate expresses
RESPECT FOR HAND TOOLS

Japanese craftsmen have a very special relationship with their tools. We believe each of our tools possesses a soul. For example, when we need to get around in our shops, we don't step over our tools; we prefer to walk around them instead.

I learned these lessons as a young apprentice in Japan, when I carried my master's toolbox for the first time. The box was made of pine, and measured about three feet long, one foot wide, and eight inches deep. Packed with steel tools, hardwood blocks, and several sharpening stones, the box was heavy enough to crush my shoulder, especially with our destination—a customer's house—still miles away. When we arrived, after struggling to keep up with my fast-walking master, I looked for a spot to put the toolbox down. Our customer, sensing the pain in my shoulder, indicated the veranda. I set the box down carelessly—and noisily. I didn't think much of it; there was nothing breakable in the box. But my master turned and yelled at me. When I looked up, I could see that he was furious. Had our customer not been there, my master probably would have struck me.

Such a scene reveals the intense experience of apprenticeships in Japan, and the setting in which I learned to respect my tools. For a *shokunin*—a craftsman with skill, speed, and professional responsibility—tools are not just things. They have a soul. They can be an extension of the craftsman's body. Japanese craftsmen form a bond with their tools, one that more closely resembles a personal relationship than one between a person and an inanimate object.

In contrast with modern methods of mechanized furniture production, working with hand tools allows you to take a personal approach to your work. When you put your mind into your work fully—as hand tools permit you to do—you give your work a human touch. Qualities like love, pride, concern, and simplicity will show in the finished work itself as by-products of the woodworking process.

There is something missing from modern furniture making. Much of it lacks warmth; it isn't personal. Fitting hundreds of inlays on a tabletop by means of a computer program may be quick, and it may be the "reasonable" way to get the job done. However, it shows nothing of the kind of feeling you impart with the keen cutting edge of a plane blade. I respect modern technology, but there has never been a greater need for hand tools as a key to express the nuances of human values.

Toshio Odate builds fine furniture in his workshop in Woodbury, Connecticut. He also teaches woodworking at the Pratt Institute in Brooklyn, New York.

MEASURING AND MARKING TOOLS

Every woodworking project begins with a single mark—a line describing the size and shape of the work's first piece. Inscribed accurately and followed skillfully, this measurement and others that follow will guide the woodcrafter unerringly toward successful completion of an object of beauty. But much is at stake: Inaccurate or erratic measurements can doom a noble design to the kindling box.

Fortunately, something close to perfection is attainable; centuries of experience have produced tools and techniques that produce reliable, accurate measurements. This chapter is a guide to those instruments and methods.

On the pages that follow you will find a wide array of instruments described; gauges of several kinds, protractors,

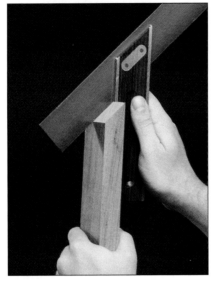

A miter square confirms that a bevel cut on the end of a board forms a 45° angle with the face. With the workpiece and square held up to the light, there should be no gap visible.

As you accumulate your tools, do not compromise on quality. Although there are genuine bargains to be found—high-quality tools at low prices—beware of cheap goods: Nothing robs the pleasure from a project more quickly than rough edges, loose joints, and hard-to-read markings.

Take the time to master the techniques of precise layout, for they—as well as the proper tools—will assure accuracy. Some details may seem inconsequential, but they are not. As explained on page 26, the position of the bevel on the tiny blade of a cutting gauge can spell the difference between cutting a groove effortlessly, and laboring endlessly to square its sides.

Even using the best measuring and marking tools and the most skilled

knives, compasses, squares, lines, tapes, and rules. Although it is possible to work well with nothing more than a pencil and ruler, each specialized tool has a job that it does better than any substitute. Some are considered indispensable. The majority of woodworkers would probably include among these a carpenter's square, a try square, a combination square, a tape measure, and a cutting gauge.

craftsmanship will not guarantee that you will always measure correctly. Eventually—and probably inevitably—you may misread your plans or miscalculate a dimension. For this reason most woodworkers take out a basic layout insurance policy: "Measure twice and cut once." Double-checking each and every mark and measurement helps ensure that you will catch your mistakes before the irreversible first cut.

A trio of marking tools works together to outline the pins for a dovetail joint. After a cutting gauge scribes a shoulder line around the end of the board, a dovetail square sets the angle for the pins on the board end. A combination square then extends the pin marks to the shoulder lines on both faces.

TOOLS FOR MEASURING AND MARKING

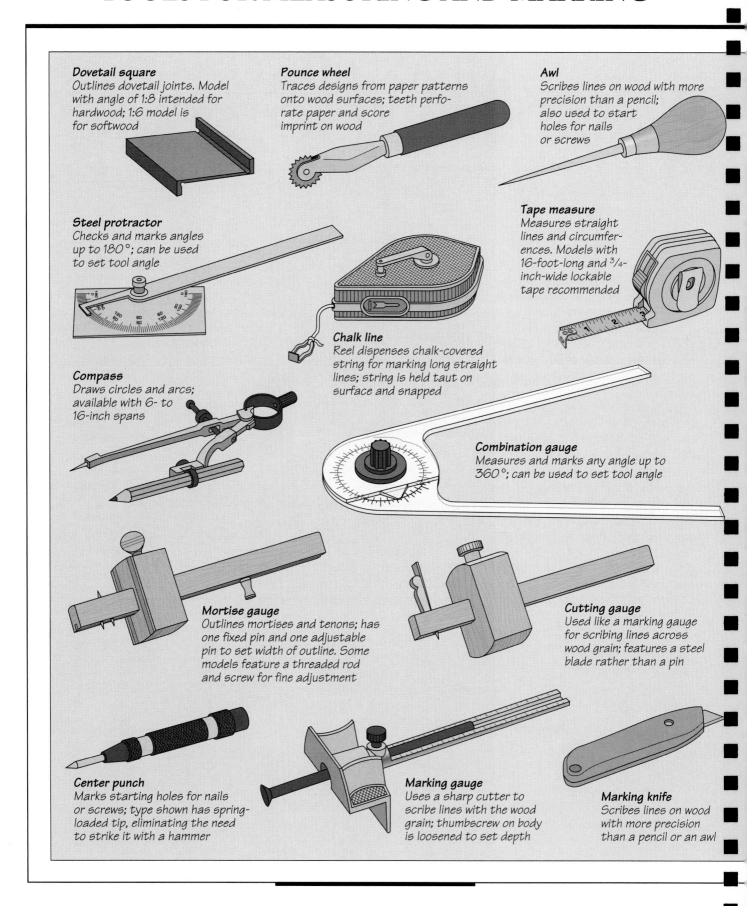

Dovetail square
Outlines dovetail joints. Model with angle of 1:8 intended for hardwood; 1:6 model is for softwood

Pounce wheel
Traces designs from paper patterns onto wood surfaces; teeth perforate paper and score imprint on wood

Awl
Scribes lines on wood with more precision than a pencil; also used to start holes for nails or screws

Steel protractor
Checks and marks angles up to 180°; can be used to set tool angle

Tape measure
Measures straight lines and circumferences. Models with 16-foot-long and 3/4-inch-wide lockable tape recommended

Chalk line
Reel dispenses chalk-covered string for marking long straight lines; string is held taut on surface and snapped

Compass
Draws circles and arcs; available with 6- to 16-inch spans

Combination gauge
Measures and marks any angle up to 360°; can be used to set tool angle

Mortise gauge
Outlines mortises and tenons; has one fixed pin and one adjustable pin to set width of outline. Some models feature a threaded rod and screw for fine adjustment

Cutting gauge
Used like a marking gauge for scribing lines across wood grain; features a steel blade rather than a pin

Center punch
Marks starting holes for nails or screws; type shown has spring-loaded tip, eliminating the need to strike it with a hammer

Marking gauge
Uses a sharp cutter to scribe lines with the wood grain; thumbscrew on body is loosened to set depth

Marking knife
Scribes lines on wood with more precision than a pencil or an awl

14

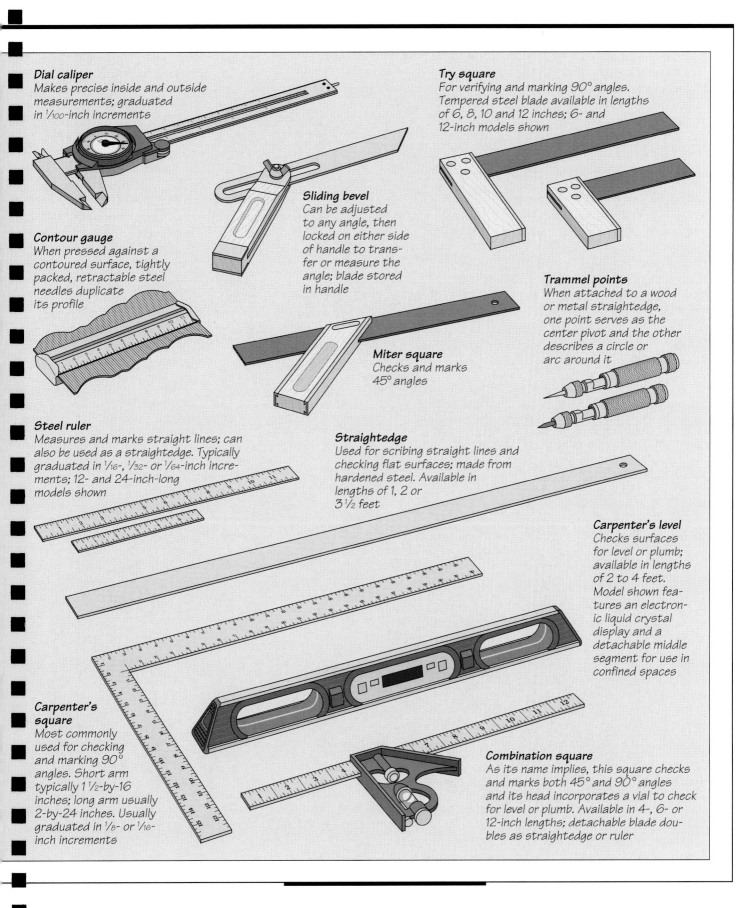

Dial caliper
Makes precise inside and outside measurements; graduated in 1/100-inch increments

Contour gauge
When pressed against a contoured surface, tightly packed, retractable steel needles duplicate its profile

Sliding bevel
Can be adjusted to any angle, then locked on either side of handle to transfer or measure the angle; blade stored in handle

Miter square
Checks and marks 45° angles

Steel ruler
Measures and marks straight lines; can also be used as a straightedge. Typically graduated in 1/16-, 1/32- or 1/64-inch increments; 12- and 24-inch-long models shown

Straightedge
Used for scribing straight lines and checking flat surfaces; made from hardened steel. Available in lengths of 1, 2 or 3 1/2 feet

Try square
For verifying and marking 90° angles. Tempered steel blade available in lengths of 6, 8, 10 and 12 inches; 6- and 12-inch models shown

Trammel points
When attached to a wood or metal straightedge, one point serves as the center pivot and the other describes a circle or arc around it

Carpenter's level
Checks surfaces for level or plumb; available in lengths of 2 to 4 feet. Model shown features an electronic liquid crystal display and a detachable middle segment for use in confined spaces

Carpenter's square
Most commonly used for checking and marking 90° angles. Short arm typically 1 1/2-by-16 inches; long arm usually 2-by-24 inches. Usually graduated in 1/8- or 1/16-inch increments

Combination square
As its name implies, this square checks and marks both 45° and 90° angles and its head incorporates a vial to check for level or plumb. Available in 4-, 6- or 12-inch lengths; detachable blade doubles as straightedge or ruler

MEASURING AND MARKING TECHNIQUES

Craftsmanship begins with proper measuring and marking. The accuracy of every line you make is only as good as the previous one. Lines that are not quite straight or angles that veer off the mark invariably result in out-of-square cuts and poorly fitting joints.

The tools shown on pages 14 and 15 are essential at many stages of a woodworking project, from initial setup to the periodic checking that you should do to confirm the progress of your work. The balance of this chapter describes some basic operations and offers a few tips and shortcuts for taking precise measurements and setting up your tools in awkward and uncommon situations.

Although useful shortcuts do exist, take nothing for granted. Experience has taught that there is even a best tool and

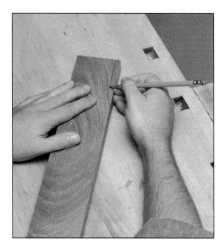

One of the simplest marking gauges is your own hand. With a pencil held between your thumb and index finger, run your middle finger along an edge of a board to mark a straight line.

technique for drawing a straight line. Sharp, medium-hard pencils, such as 2H, or a fine-point mechanical pencil, are best for thin and clean lines; softer-tipped pencils like HB produce wider lines that can introduce inaccuracy. Hold a pencil at a slight angle to the surface being marked so that the point rides along the edge of your ruler. The best markers have beveled edges, so that the graduation mark is close to the work surface. If you are working with a square-sided ruler, hold it on edge to avoid any distortion. If you are laying out a precision joint, a marking knife will produce a finer line than a pencil.

A safety reminder: If your measuring or marking involves a power tool, make sure the machine is unplugged while you set it up.

LINES AND ANGLES

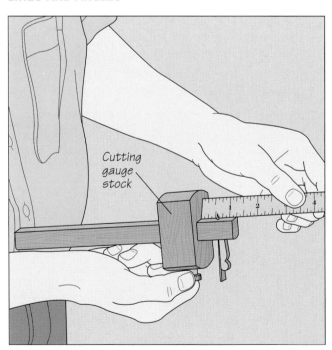

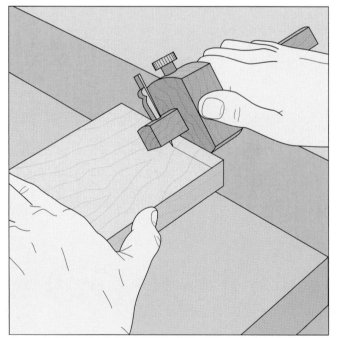

Scribing a line
To mark a line across the end of a board, use a cutting gauge. Loosen the thumbscrew on the gauge and use a ruler to set the distance between the blade and the tool's stock. Tighten the thumbscrew *(above, left)*. You can tap the stock with a finger to move it slightly. Then, holding the board flat on a work surface, butt the stock against its end and guide the blade across the surface *(above, right)*. Holding the gauge on an angle will make a clean, straight cut.

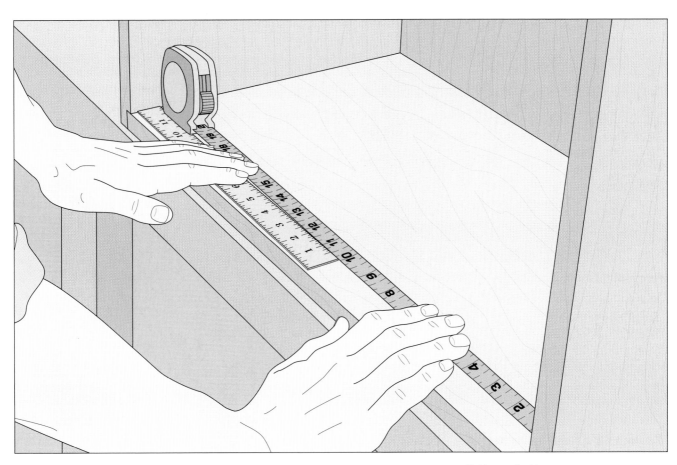

Taking an inside measurement
The length of a tape measure case as marked on its side or bottom is not always accurate, so you should not rely on the tool alone to make an inside measurement. A better method is to use a tape measure in conjunction with a ruler. To determine the distance between the side panels of a carcase, butt the ruler against one panel and the end of the tape against the other panel; butt the tape measure up against the ruler to ensure that both tools are measuring along the same line *(above)*. To calculate the distance, read the tape marking just where the tape contacts the ruler, then add it to the length of the ruler.

SHOP TIP

Inside measurement using two sticks
Two straight and square sticks can serve as accurate gauges for measuring inside distances. Place the sticks side by side in the enclosed space, butting one stick against one edge and the other against the opposite edge. Mark a line across the sticks, then remove them and realign the marks. The combined length of the sticks will give you the inside measurement.

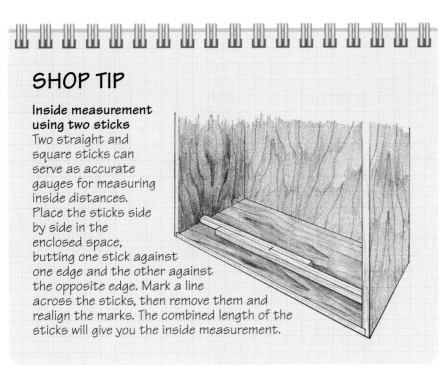

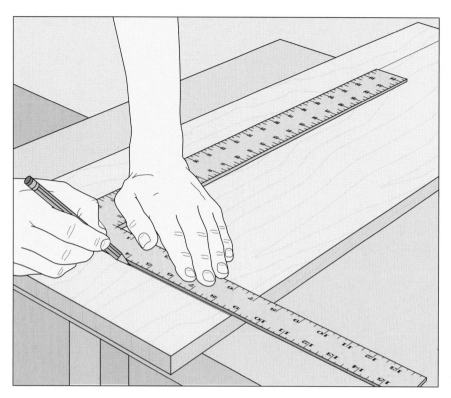

Marking a line perpendicular to an existing line
If your workpiece is too wide or long for a try square or combination square, use a carpenter's square. Align the outer edge of the square's long arm with the existing line, then draw a pencil line along the short arm *(left)*.

Marking a line at an angle to an edge
Set the angle you need on a metal protractor, then unscrew the wing nut of a sliding bevel to loosen the blade. Holding the inner edge of the blade against the base of the protractor, align the bevel's handle with the protractor dial, then tighten the wing nut *(right)*. To transfer the angle, hold the bevel's handle against the edge of the workpiece and draw a pencil line along the blade *(inset)*.

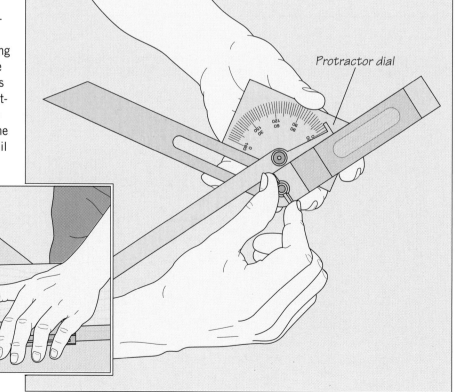

Protractor dial

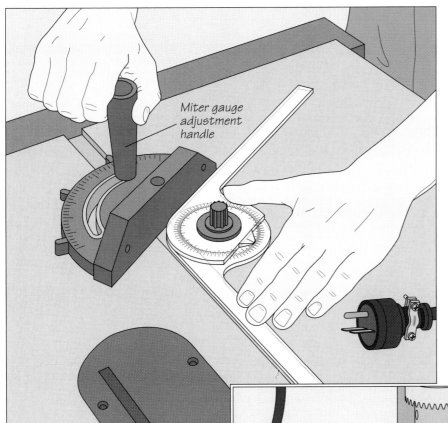

Miter gauge adjustment handle

Setting up a table saw for a miter cut
Set the desired miter angle on a combination gauge, then loosen the adjustment handle on the saw's miter gauge. Align one arm of the combination gauge with the miter slot in the saw table and swivel the miter head to bring it flush against the other arm. Tighten the adjustment handle on the gauge *(left)*. To check a 45° angle miter cut, use a combination square *(page 20)*.

Adjusting a drill press to bore an angled hole
Install a straight steel rod or a brad-point bit in the chuck of the drill press, then use a protractor to set the drilling angle you need on a sliding bevel *(page 18)*. Loosen the table, butt the bevel's blade against the rod or bit and tilt the table up until it rests flush against the handle of the bevel *(right)*. Tighten the table. (Because of the design of its shaft, a brad-point bit provides more flat surface to butt a bevel blade against than does a regular twist bit.)

Checking a 45° miter cut

To confirm that the cut end of a workpiece forms a 45° angle with the edge, use a combination square. Holding the square up to the light, butt its 45° face against the edge of the workpiece and set the blade against the cut end *(right)*. If the angle is correct, no light will be visible between blade and board.

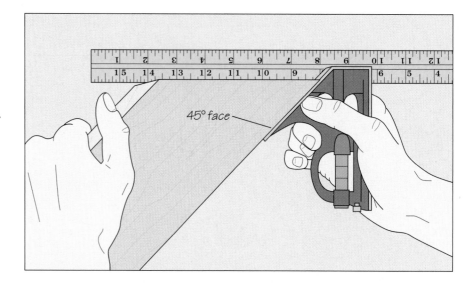

45° face

Bisecting an angle

Use a compass to divide an angle into two equal parts. With the legs of the tool a few inches apart, position the pivot point at the apex of the angle and swivel the compass to make a reference mark on each arm of the angle. (In the illustration, the edge of the panel serves as one arm of the angle.) Then make two more reference marks: This time, position the pivot point at the intersection of one of the first two marks and the arm of the angle; repeat for the other arm of the angle. The new reference marks should cross between the arms of the angle *(right)*. Bisect the angle by drawing a straight line from the apex of the angle to the intersection of the last two reference marks *(inset)*.

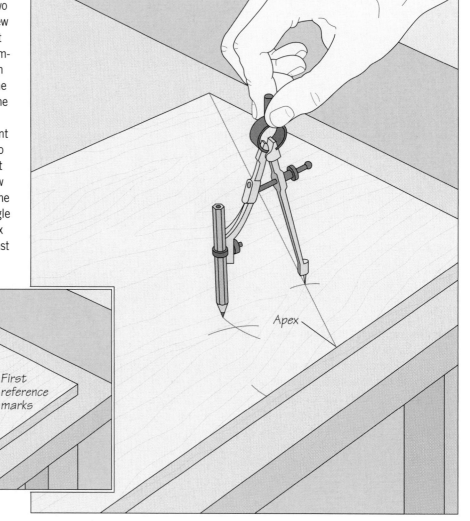

Apex

Second set of reference marks

First reference marks

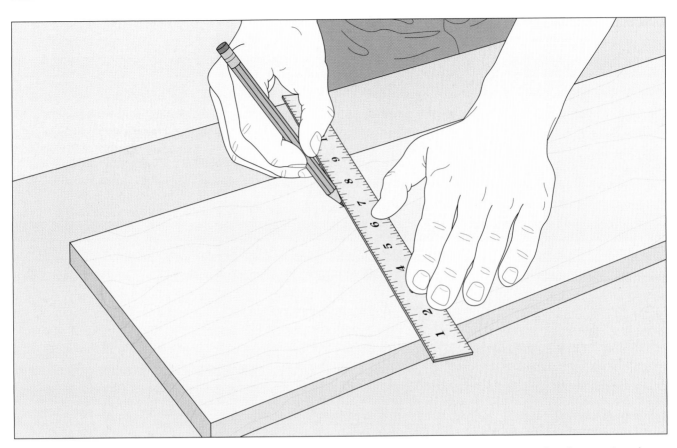

Dividing a workpiece into equal sections

To divide a surface whose width is not easily divisible into equal segments—for example, a 7⁷⁄₁₆-inch-wide board into four divisions—use a ruler and pencil. Position the 1-inch mark of the ruler at one edge of the workpiece and angle the tool until you have a measurement that can be divided easily by 4—in this case, 8 inches—with the other edge of the board. Then use a pencil to make a mark every 2 inches along the ruler *(above)*; the marks will be exactly the same distance apart, dividing the surface into four equal segments.

SHOP TIP

Checking a try square
To confirm whether a try square is true, hold the handle against the edge of a straight board and draw a pencil along the blade.
Then turn over the square.
The edge of the blade
should lie right on top
of the marked line.
Any difference
between the
two represents
twice the error
of the square.
You can also
use this technique
to check a carpen-
ter's square.

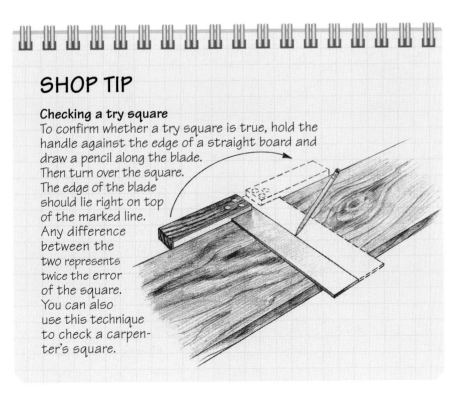

CIRCLES AND CURVES

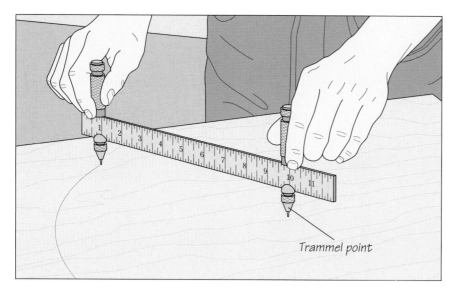

Trammel point

Marking a circle

To scribe a circle with a radius greater than the span of a compass or dividers, use a set of trammel points. Install a sharpened pencil lead in one of the points and use a ruler to set the gap between the points equal to the radius of the circle you need to draw. On the type shown, slide the trammel points to the appropriate position along the ruler, and tighten the thumbscrews. Then hold the pivot point steady at the center of the circle and slowly rotate the pencil point around it *(left)*.

BUILD IT YOURSELF

A SHOP-MADE COMPASS

The shop-made compass shown at right, consisting of an arm, an awl, and a pencil, will allow you to scribe a circle of virtually any radius. For the arm, cut a strip of ½-inch stock 2 inches wide and at least 2 inches longer than the radius of the circle you wish to draw. Bore a hole about 1 inch from the end of the arm, large enough to hold the shaft of the awl. Bore a second hole, wide enough to accommodate the pencil, making the distance between the holes equal to the radius of the circle. Fit the awl into one hole and a sharpened pencil into the other, making sure the two extend from the bottom of the arm by the same amount.

Use the compass as you would trammel points, holding the tip of the awl at the center of the circle and rotating the pencil around it to scribe the circle.

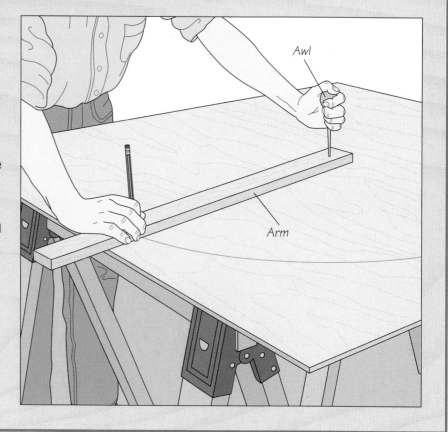

Awl

Arm

Transferring a design onto a template

A pounce wheel will enable you to transfer a design from paper to a rigid template. Tape the sheet of paper on the template and carefully trace along the outline of the design with the pounce wheel *(right)*, pressing hard enough to make an impression on the template. The wheel will punch tiny marks on the template surface. To make the marks more visible, place a sheet of carbon paper between the paper and the template or sprinkle some chalk powder along the design outline on the paper. The wheel points will press the chalk through to the template.

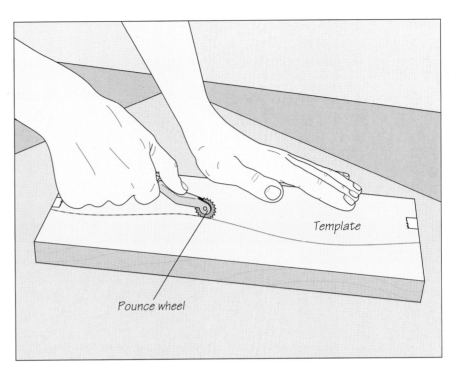

Template

Pounce wheel

Locating the center of a circular piece

The center-finding jig shown at left consists of a combination square and a carpenter's square clamped together. To set up the jig, join the two squares so that the blade of the combination square extends through the center of the 90° angle formed by the arms of the carpenter's square. To use the jig, set the workpiece flat on a work surface and position the device so that the arms of the carpenter's square contact the piece along its circumference. Mark a line on the surface of the workpiece along the blade of the combination square, then rotate the workpiece and draw a second line *(left)*. The two lines will intersect at the center of the circle.

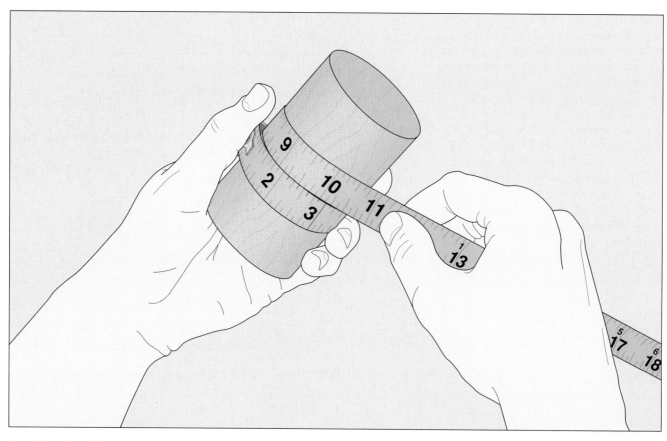

Measuring circumference

To determine the circumference of a cylindrical or circular workpiece, wrap a length of measuring tape around its girth and hold it taut so that two sections of the tape are side-by-side on the surface *(above)*. Choose two marks that line up—for example, the 2- and 9⅛-inch marks. The difference between the two will give you the circumference—in this case, 7⅛ inches.

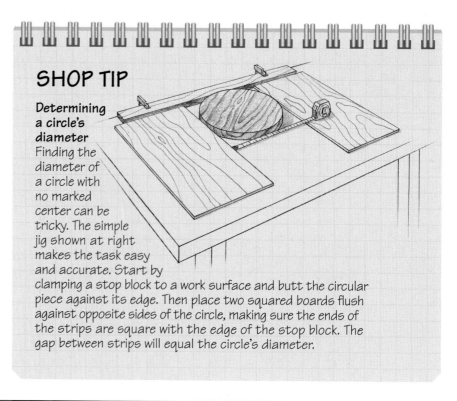

SHOP TIP

Determining a circle's diameter
Finding the diameter of a circle with no marked center can be tricky. The simple jig shown at right makes the task easy and accurate. Start by clamping a stop block to a work surface and butt the circular piece against its edge. Then place two squared boards flush against opposite sides of the circle, making sure the ends of the strips are square with the edge of the stop block. The gap between strips will equal the circle's diameter.

MARKING JOINTS

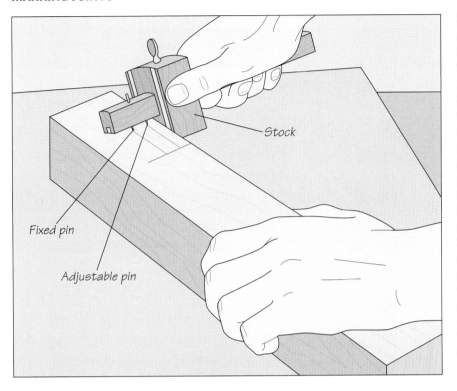

Stock

Fixed pin

Adjustable pin

Outlining a mortise

Adjust a mortise gauge so that the gap between its fixed and adjustable pins is the same as the width of the mortise you need. If you have already cut the tenon, use its width to set up the gauge; otherwise, you may wish to use the blade width of the chisel you will use to chop out the mortise as a guide. To mark the mortise at the appropriate point on your workpiece, position the stock of the gauge so that the gap between it and the adjustable pin equals the gap between the edge of the workpiece and the mortise location. On the type shown, loosen the thumbscrew on the stock and slide it to the correct position along the handle. To mark the mortise, guide the gauge along the surface of the workpiece while holding the stock flush against the edge *(left)*. The pins will scribe the sides of the mortise outline in the wood.

BUILD IT YOURSELF

A FIXED-WIDTH MORTISE GAUGE

The mortise gauge shown at right can be made in the shop from a small wood block, a dowel, and a piece of metal. Refer to the illustration for suggested dimensions. To make the handle, saw the dowel to length and cut a thin ¾-inch-long kerf into one end on a band saw. Then make the cutter from a piece of hacksaw blade slightly longer than the width of the dowel and as wide as the mortise you need to mark. Grind one end to two points and cut a notch in each side. Fit the cutter in the kerf, then drive two finishing nails into the dowel, aligning them with the notches to hold the cutter securely *(above)*. Cut the stock of the

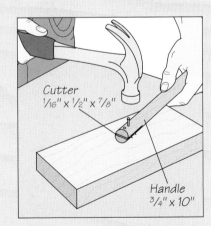

Cutter
1/16" x 1/2" x 7/8"

Handle
3/4" x 10"

gauge to size and bore two holes into it: the first one through its center for the dowel and the second one into the top through to the first hole for a screw. Slide the dowel through

the hole in the block. File the screw tip flat and drive it into the second hole to hold the stock steady on the dowel handle. Use the gauge in the same way as a commercial model *(below)*.

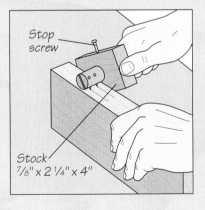

Stop screw

Stock
7/8" x 2 1/4" x 4"

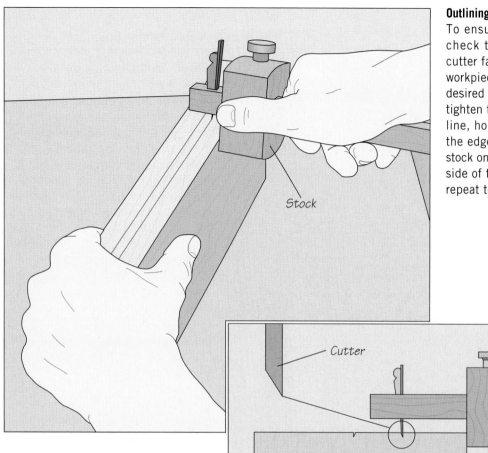

Stock

Outlining a groove with a cutting gauge
To ensure that the groove is square, check that the beveled edge of the cutter faces toward the middle of the workpiece *(inset)*. Set the gauge to the desired position of one side of the cut, tighten the thumbscrew, and scribe the line, holding the stock firmly against the edge of the work. Reposition the stock on the gauge handle for the other side of the groove if necessary, then repeat to cut the second mark *(left)*.

Cutter

Checking the depth of a rabbet
To measure the depth of a rabbet accurately, use a combination square. Set the 90° face of the square against the surface of the workpiece adjoining the rabbet. Then loosen the lock nut on the handle and slide the blade down so that it contacts the bottom of the rabbet. Tighten the lock nut and read the marking on the blade *(right)*.

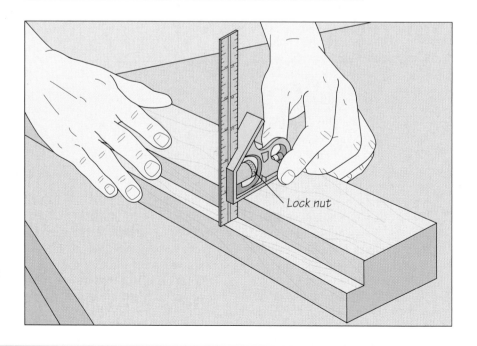

Lock nut

CHECKING FOR SQUARE

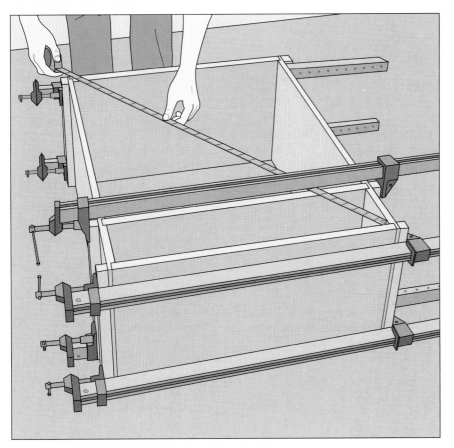

Measuring the diagonals
To determine whether a cabinet carcase is square before gluing, measure the diagonals between opposite corners immediately after tightening the clamps *(left)*. The two results should be the same. If not, the carcase is out of square. To correct the problem, install another bar clamp across the longer of the two diagonals. Tighten the clamp a little at a time, measuring as you go until the two diagonals are equal.

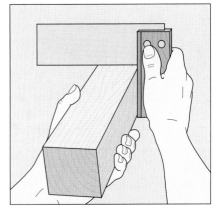

Checking a board for square
Use a try square to check whether a surface forms a 90° angle with an adjoining side. With the workpiece and the square held up to the light, hold the handle flush against the adjoining surface and the blade across the surface to be tested *(above)*. There should be no gap visible between the blade and the workpiece. If there is, the surface is not square.

SHOP TIP

Truing a carpenter's square
If your carpenter's square is out of square *(page 21)*, you can true it with a center punch and a ball-peen hammer. Begin by marking a straight line between the inside and outside corners of the square. If the angle formed by the square is greater than 90°, you will need to move the arms closer together: Place the tip of the punch on the line near the square's outside corner and tap it with the hammer. If the angle is less than 90°, spread the arms apart by tapping on the line near the square's inside corner, as shown here. Truing a square may require several taps, but check your progress after each attempt.

HANDSAWS

Its blade held taut by a tensioning wire, a frame saw slices through a hardwood board. Because frame saw blades are thinner than most other saw blades, they seldom bind—even in long rip cuts.

The handsaw has a rich history that began at least 4,000 years ago, when the Egyptians fashioned saw blades from copper and joined them to pistol-grip handles. Later, the Greeks and Romans devised frames that held blades tautly in place. They also discovered the importance of setting saw teeth—bending them alternately to the right and left—so the saw cuts a kerf slightly wider than the blade. The design is still used today to prevent a blade from binding in the cut.

Medieval craftsmen tinkered with the design of the frame, but it was not until the 17th Century that handsaws assumed their modern guise when English saw manufacturers attached a wooden handle with an oval hand hole to a steel blade. Tool design flourished and within 100 years, cabinetmakers devised tenon and dovetail saws by adding a heavy steel or brass spine to a shorter, finer, smaller-toothed blade. Today, there is a handsaw for just about any cutting task.

Although all handsaws cut wood in the same way, there are important differences between them. As discussed on page 32, the number of teeth on a blade, their shape and the spacing between them, all affect a saw's performance. The finely spaced teeth of a dovetail saw, for example, allow it to cut wood cleanly and its reinforced back keeps the blade from bending when making a cut. Both characteristics are required to meet the strict tolerances of a dovetail joint. But such a saw would be useless for a long rip cut; this is better handled by a long blade with widely spaced teeth filed to an aggressive cutting angle. For sawing a curve, yet another tool is required, like the bowsaw or coping saw, which can follow intricate cutting lines. Even the work of a specialized saw is enhanced by the use of a simple jig. Devices like the crosscutting jigs shown on page 37 will ensure more accurate cuts—and save you time too.

While few woodworkers would want to dispense with their electric saws, handsaws offer some appealing advantages. They are safer, quieter, more portable, and easier to maintain than their power counterparts. A good-quality handsaw can last a lifetime with periodic sharpening; even one that has been neglected for decades can be reconditioned, provided the blade is unpitted and reasonably rust-free. Sharpening is done easily with a vise, a file, a saw set, and the proper technique shown starting on page 32. But delicate saw blades with finer teeth, like those of a coping or fret saw, are simply replaced when they become dull.

A bowsaw is the ideal tool for cutting curves in wood. The blade can be set at virtually any angle in its frame, enabling it to follow the intricate cutting path characteristic of decorative scrollwork.

HANDSAW INVENTORY

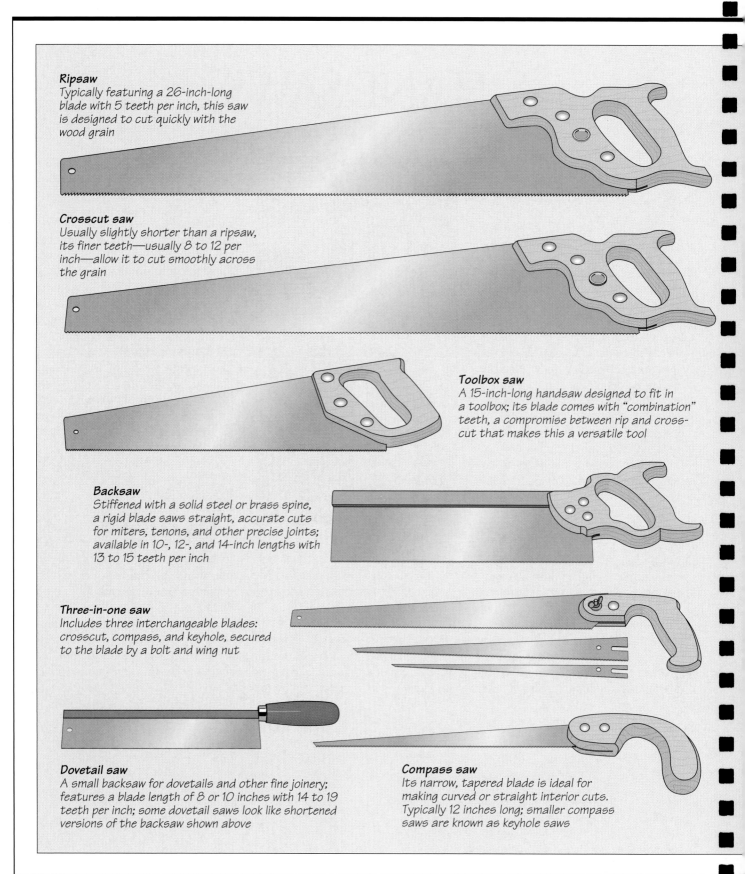

Ripsaw
Typically featuring a 26-inch-long blade with 5 teeth per inch, this saw is designed to cut quickly with the wood grain

Crosscut saw
Usually slightly shorter than a ripsaw, its finer teeth—usually 8 to 12 per inch—allow it to cut smoothly across the grain

Toolbox saw
A 15-inch-long handsaw designed to fit in a toolbox; its blade comes with "combination" teeth, a compromise between rip and cross-cut that makes this a versatile tool

Backsaw
Stiffened with a solid steel or brass spine, a rigid blade saws straight, accurate cuts for miters, tenons, and other precise joints; available in 10-, 12-, and 14-inch lengths with 13 to 15 teeth per inch

Three-in-one saw
Includes three interchangeable blades: crosscut, compass, and keyhole, secured to the blade by a bolt and wing nut

Dovetail saw
A small backsaw for dovetails and other fine joinery; features a blade length of 8 or 10 inches with 14 to 19 teeth per inch; some dovetail saws look like shortened versions of the backsaw shown above

Compass saw
Its narrow, tapered blade is ideal for making curved or straight interior cuts. Typically 12 inches long; smaller compass saws are known as keyhole saws

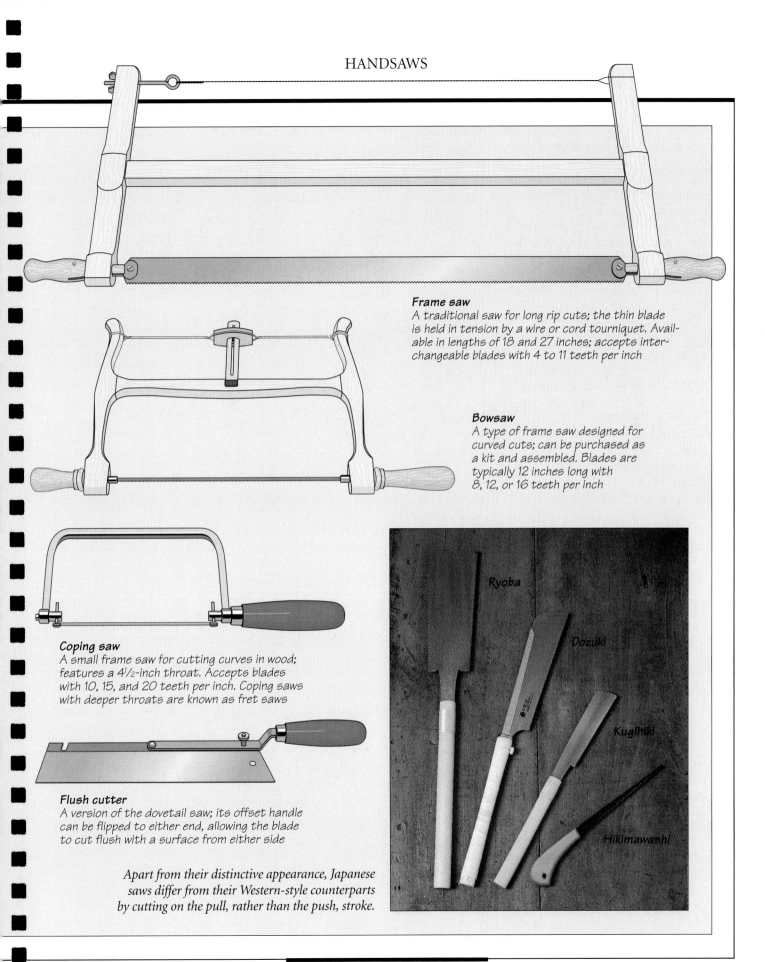

Frame saw
A traditional saw for long rip cuts; the thin blade is held in tension by a wire or cord tourniquet. Available in lengths of 18 and 27 inches; accepts interchangeable blades with 4 to 11 teeth per inch

Bowsaw
A type of frame saw designed for curved cuts; can be purchased as a kit and assembled. Blades are typically 12 inches long with 8, 12, or 16 teeth per inch

Coping saw
A small frame saw for cutting curves in wood; features a 4 1/2-inch throat. Accepts blades with 10, 15, and 20 teeth per inch. Coping saws with deeper throats are known as fret saws

Flush cutter
A version of the dovetail saw; its offset handle can be flipped to either end, allowing the blade to cut flush with a surface from either side

Apart from their distinctive appearance, Japanese saws differ from their Western-style counterparts by cutting on the pull, rather than the push, stroke.

Ryoba

Dozuki

Kugihiki

Hikimawashi

HANDSAW BLADES

All saw blades are essentially alike, consisting of a row of sharp teeth that sever wood fibers and clear the resulting debris out of the cut, or kerf. But blades intended for different uses deviate markedly in their details.

A ripsaw blade has widely spaced teeth—five to seven teeth per inch (TPI)—designed to tear rapidly along the grain. To speed the work and prevent binding, rip teeth have a pronounced "set," that is, they are bent alternately to each side of the blade's center line. The resulting edge, although relatively rough, can easily be planed smooth.

A crosscut saw, on the other hand, must make precise cuts, usually only a few inches long. Its teeth are closely spaced—eight to 12 TPI—and possess barely any set; although they cut slowly, little cleanup is necessary.

Of course, no saw cuts well if its teeth are not sharpened and set properly. For the most part, these tasks can be done in the shop *(see below)*, although saws with very fine teeth, like dovetails and tenon saws, are best left to professionals.

A CLOSE-UP VIEW OF HANDSAW TEETH

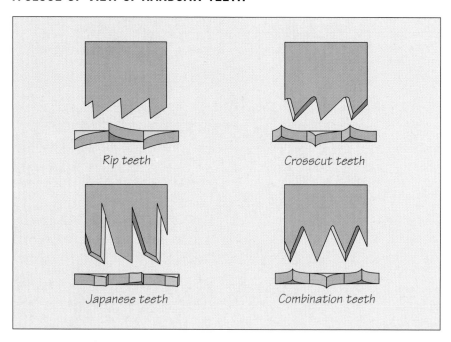

Rip teeth

Crosscut teeth

Japanese teeth

Combination teeth

Four types of teeth

Handsaw teeth are shaped according to the type of cutting they will do. The leading edges of ripsaw teeth are almost vertical and filed straight across to enable them to slash aggressively through wood. Crosscut saw teeth have sloped leading edges that are beveled, which allow them to cut cleanly across the grain. Japanese saw teeth cut on the pull stroke. They are relatively tall and narrow, and feature a bevel across the top of the cutting points. Unlike Western-style saw teeth, Japanese teeth have very little set and produce a narrow kerf. Combination, or dual-purpose, teeth slope forward and backward at the same angle, and are beveled on both edges. Although they rip more slowly than a ripsaw, and produce crosscuts that are rougher than a specialized crosscutting saw, combination saws do both jobs.

SHARPENING SAW TEETH

1 Jointing the teeth
Mount the saw teeth-up in a vise with a wood pad on either side of the blade for protection. Install a flat mill bastard file in a commercial saw jointer. Holding the jointer flush against one side of the blade, pass the file back and forth along the tips of the teeth *(right)*. The file will flatten the tips of any high teeth slightly; a few passes should be enough to file all the teeth to the same height.

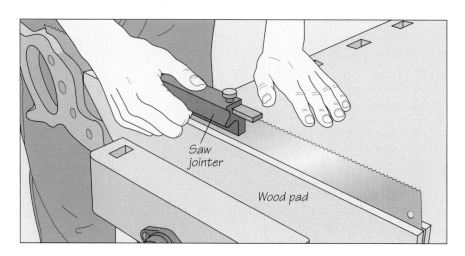

Saw jointer

Wood pad

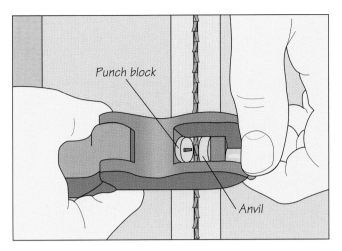

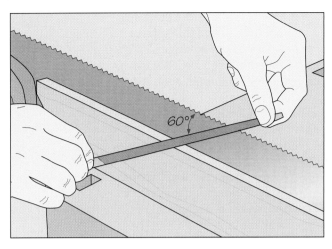

2 Setting the teeth

With the saw still in the vise, adjust a saw set to the same TPI as the blade. Starting at the tip, or toe-end, of the saw, position the first tooth that is bent to the right between the anvil and the punch block. Squeeze the handle to set the tooth *(above)*. Work your way toward the handle, setting all teeth that are bent to the right. Then turn the saw around in the vise and repeat the operation to set the remaining teeth.

3 Filing the teeth

To form the bevel required on crosscut saw teeth, hold a slim-taper triangular file at a 60° angle to the blade with its handle tilted down slightly *(above)*. For ripsaw teeth, the file should remain perpendicular to the blade. As you file the teeth, work from the toe to the handle, shaping all the teeth that are set in one direction. Then turn the saw around to shape the remaining teeth.

BUILD IT YOURSELF

A JOINTING JIG FOR SAW TEETH

The jig shown at right is as effective as a commercial saw jointer for leveling the teeth of a handsaw, yet you can make it from just three wood scraps: a top and two sides. Saw the pieces to the dimensions suggested in the illustration, then cut a groove in the bottom face of the top piece wide and deep enough to hold a flat mill bastard file snugly. Bevel the top corners of the two side pieces to fit the saw teeth. Screw the side pieces to the top, spacing them far enough apart to clear the saw blade, but close enough to keep the file perpendicular to the blade as you joint the teeth.

To use the jig, slide a file into the groove in the top piece and pass it along the saw teeth as you would with a commercial jointer.

BASIC CUTS

S awing wood quickly and accurately by hand depends on the proper set-up, posture, and sawing angle. Always support a workpiece adequately, either on sawhorses or some other stable surface, and keep it in place with clamps or a vise. Never attempt to steady a workpiece with your free hand.

Set up your work at a comfortable height that allows you to maintain your balance while sawing. Hold the saw blade in line with your arm and shoulder. As shown below, the correct sawing angle varies with the type of cut. The saw is held closest to the vertical for rip cuts, and somewhat lower for crosscutting. An even lower angle will yield the finest cut. As illustrated in the photo at right, to finish off an interior cut, you have to hold the saw with the blade at a 90° angle to the surface.

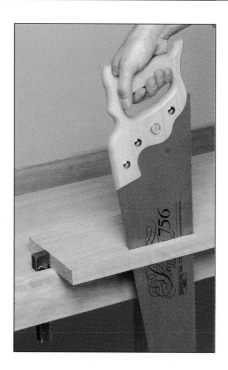

If, in spite of your preparations, the saw drifts off the cutting line, twist the blade slightly on the push stroke to straighten it out. If the blade sticks during the cut, you may need to reset or file the teeth *(page 32)*. As a short-term measure, you can rub a little paste wax or paraffin on the blade (not the teeth) or use a kerf splitter to keep the blade from sticking *(page 35)*. Remove any wax buildup with steel wool and mineral spirits.

When you measure and mark a cut, remember that the kerf will be up to ⅛ inch wide. Be sure to make your cut on the waste side of the cutting line.

Holding a saw vertically at the end of an interior cut enables the teeth to end the cut square.

SAWING ANGLES

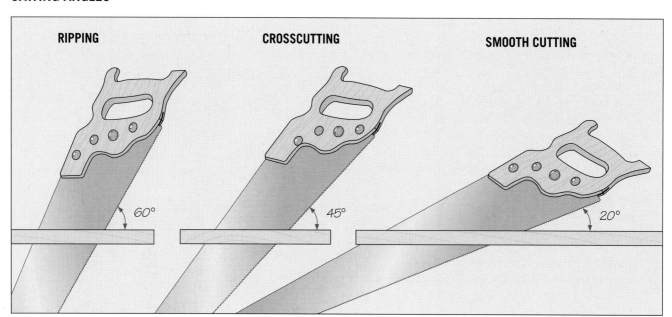

RIPPING   60°

CROSSCUTTING   45°

SMOOTH CUTTING   20°

Choosing the right angle
Although holding a saw at a 90° angle to the workpiece, as shown in the photo above, is the quickest way to shear through wood, the resulting cut edges are invariably rough and splintered. For finer cuts, lower the angle of the saw. Start the operation with as low an angle as possible, then raise the angle, to about 60° for rip cuts and to about 45° for crosscuts. To completely eliminate rough edges and splintering, keep the saw at an angle of about 20° to the workpiece.

RIPPING

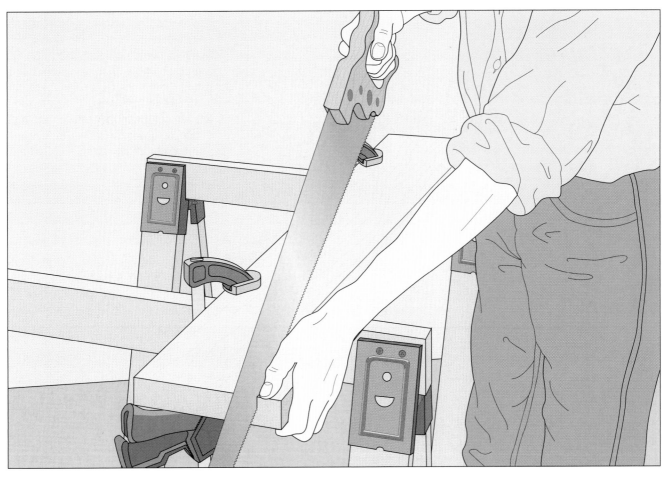

Sawing a long board to width
Clamp the workpiece to sawhorses. To start the cut, position the saw blade to the waste side of the cutting line and set your thumb next to the blade. Pull the blade slowly toward you, keeping it flush against your thumb *(above)*. Repeat a few times until the kerf is deep enough to hold the blade, then move your thumb out of the way and continue the cut. Saw with slow, steady strokes using the full length of the blade; reposition the workpiece on the sawhorses as necessary.

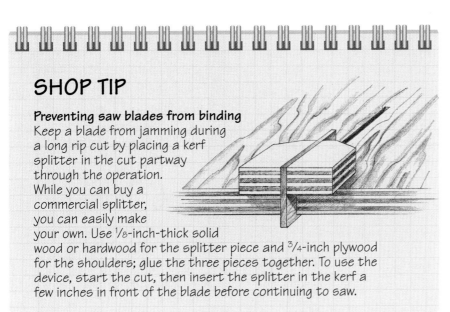

SHOP TIP

Preventing saw blades from binding
Keep a blade from jamming during a long rip cut by placing a kerf splitter in the cut partway through the operation. While you can buy a commercial splitter, you can easily make your own. Use ⅛-inch-thick solid wood or hardwood for the splitter piece and ¾-inch plywood for the shoulders; glue the three pieces together. To use the device, start the cut, then insert the splitter in the kerf a few inches in front of the blade before continuing to saw.

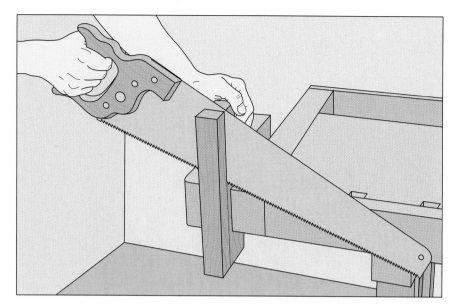

Ripping a short board
Secure the workpiece vertically in a vise with the cutting line extending from the vise; this will keep the workpiece from rattling and the saw blade from binding. Start the cut normally, using your free hand to steady the piece once the blade is completely in the kerf. To minimize tearout, straighten the blade until it is nearly perpendicular to the face as you near the end of the cut.

CROSSCUTTING

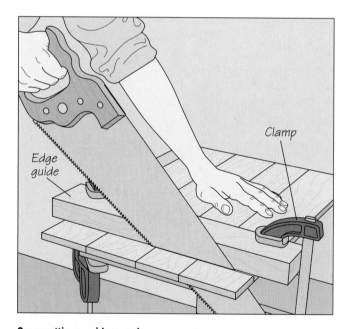

Cutting a board to length
Clamp the workpiece to sawhorses. Start the operation as you would a rip cut *(page 35)*, then lower the saw to an angle of about 45° once the kerf is deep enough. Saw slowly and steadily with the full length of the blade. To prevent the waste piece from tearing the wood as you complete the cut, support the waste with your free hand while raising the angle of the blade until it is almost vertical.

Crosscutting a wide panel
Set the panel on a work surface with the cutting line extending off the table. To help you keep the saw blade vertical and prevent it from veering off-line during the cut, clamp a board as a edge guide to the workpiece on the good side of the cutting line. The guide should be longer than the width of the panel and square with its edges. Set up the clamps so that they will not interfere with the saw as you make the cut. Saw through the panel as you would a standard crosscut, keeping the blade flush against the guide throughout the operation *(above)*.

BUILD IT YOURSELF

TWO CROSSCUTTING JIGS

The shop-built jigs shown at right and below will ensure that your crosscuts are square; each is designed for use with a different work surface—a workbench or saw horses.

For the bench hook jig *(right)*, use ½-inch plywood for the edge guide and strips of 2-by-2 stock for the lips. Make the edge guide at least as long as the width of your workpiece and wide enough to support it. Screw the lips to the guide, attaching one to each face. Take care to align the lips flush with opposite ends of the guide.

To use the jig, butt one lip against the edge of your bench and press the workpiece firmly against the other lip. Align the cutting line with the edge of the guide and make the cut, keeping

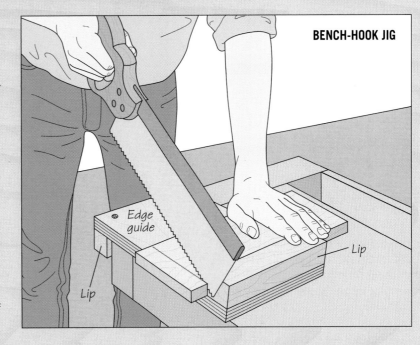

BENCH-HOOK JIG

Edge guide

Lip

Lip

CROSS-CUTTING GUIDE

the blade against the guide and steadying the jig with your free hand.

Another type of crosscutting guide *(left)*, for use with a sawhorse, is built with ¾-inch plywood. Cut the base and fence longer than the width of your workpiece. Screw the fence and lip to the base, then clamp the jig to the stock, butting the lip against the edge of the workpiece and aligning the fence with the cutting line. Keep the blade flush against the fence as you make the cut.

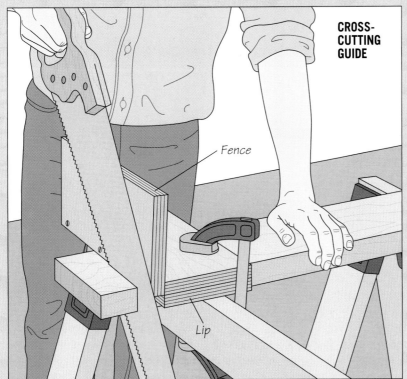

Fence

Lip

BUILD IT YOURSELF

A SIZING BOARD FOR CROSSCUTS

To crosscut several workpieces to the same length, use a shop-built sizing board like the one shown at right. The jig features an adjustable stop block that can be positioned at any distance from a kerf in the fence.

Cut the base and fence to the dimensions suggested in the illustration from ½- or ¾-inch plywood. Use hardwood for the stop block and lip. Screw the lip to the underside of the base, taking care to align the edges of the two pieces. Saw the fence into two segments about 7 inches from one end, then use a router to cut grooves through both pieces about 1 inch from their top edges; stop the grooves about 2 inches from the ends of each piece. Make the width of the grooves equal to the diameter of a 1½-inch-long, ¼-inch-diameter carriage bolt. Screw the two fence sections to the base, ensuring that the gap between the two pieces is wide enough to accommodate your saw blade. Saw a kerf across the surface of the base in line with the kerf in the fence.

To prepare the stop block, cut a 3-inch-long rabbet on one face and bore a clearance hole through its center for the carriage bolt. Fasten the block to the fence with the bolt, washer, and wing nut.

To use the sizing board, butt the lip against the edge of a workbench. Then loosen the wing nut and slide the stop block along the fence to the proper distance from the kerf between the two fences. Tighten the wing nut and butt the

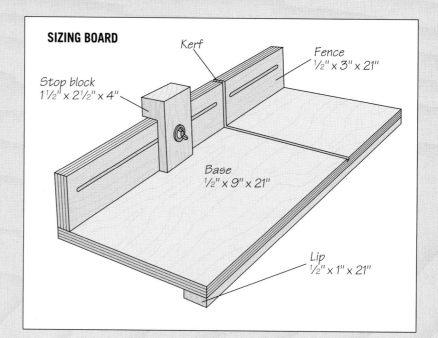

SIZING BOARD

Kerf

Fence
½" x 3" x 21"

Stop block
1½" x 2½" x 4"

Base
½" x 9" x 21"

Lip
½" x 1" x 21"

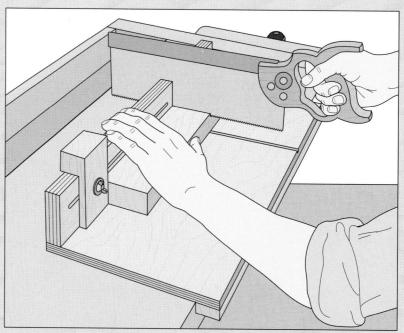

end of the workpiece against the stop block. Hold the stock firmly against the fence as you saw, using the kerf as a guide *(below)*.

ANGLE CUTS

Cutting a miter

If you are using the type of miter box shown, screw its legs to a ³/₄-inch plywood base and secure the base to a work surface. Then loosen the locking knob and swivel the saw assembly until the pointer indicates the miter angle you need. Tighten the knob. Raise the saw assembly on the guide posts high enough to slip the workpiece under the blade and set it on the base of the miter box. Align the cutting line with the blade and butt the workpiece against the fence, then lower the blade onto the workpiece. Holding the stock firmly in position, tilt the handle-end of the saw assembly down slightly, then start the cut by pulling the assembly toward you a few times. Continue the cut with steady push and pull strokes, gradually raising the handle until the blade is horizontal *(right)*.

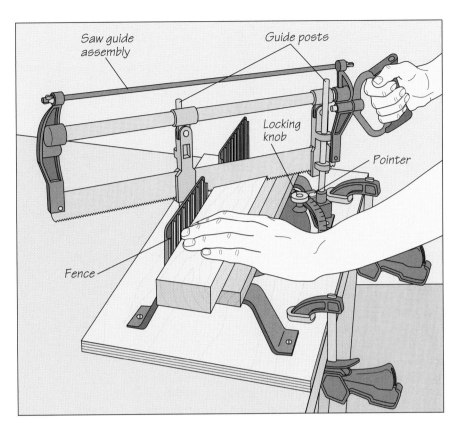

Cutting a bevel

Secure the miter box in a vise, then set your workpiece on the base of the box, aligning the cutting line with the bevel slot. Tighten the clamps in the box to hold the board in position. Slip the blade of a backsaw into the slot and cut the bevel as you would a miter *(left)*.

BUILD IT YOURSELF

MITER BOX

Start by cutting three 15-inch-long pieces of hardwood for the base and the front and back pieces. Make the base wide enough for the stock you will be sawing, and cut a plywood back-up board to protect the base. Rip the front and back pieces so that the depth of the box will be ½ inch less than the width of your backsaw blade from its teeth to the bottom of the spine. Cut the front piece 1 inch wider than the back piece to form a lip. Screw the front and back pieces to the base so that the top edges of the box are level.

Use a combination square to mark cutting lines for the slots on the top edges of the box. Lay out a 90° angle slot 2 inches from one end, and a 45° angle slot 2 inches from the other end. Outline a second 45° slot in the opposite direction between the first two slots. Cut the slots with

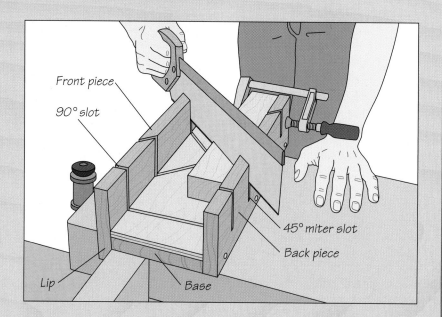

a backsaw, using blocks clamped to either side of the cutting lines to guide the blade.

To use the box, secure the lip in a vise, then set the workpiece on

the base, aligning the cutting line with the appropriate slot. Clamp the board to the front piece *(above)* and make the cut as you would with a commercial miter box.

SHOP TIP

Protecting saw blade teeth
Shield your saw blade teeth from damage when they are not in use by covering them with a protective sheath. Cut a narrow slot in a thin piece of hardwood *(top)* or rigid foam *(middle)*, then drive two screws on either side of the groove; use wire to hold the wood or foam snugly against the blade. Alternatively, cut an old garden hose *(bottom)* to the appropriate length and slit the piece to fit it over the blade.

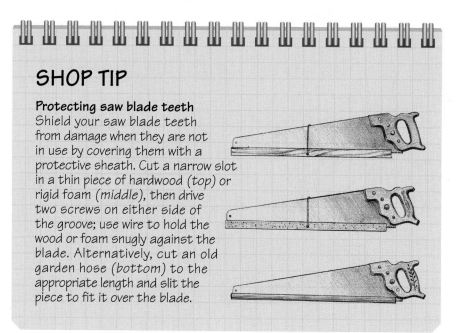

Some sawing tasks cannot be done with standard handsaws. Cutting an intricate curve or trimming a workpiece flush with an adjoining surface, for example, demands specialty saws like those shown on the following pages.

Gentle curves and rectangular interior cuts can be made with a compass saw. Tighter contours, however, require a saw with the thinnest of blades, held under tension to prevent it from bending and breaking.

Bowsaws and coping saws are types of frame saws capable of cutting complicated curves while leaving a narrow kerf. Both feature blades that can be rotated in the frame for cuts that are deeper than the throat of the saw. They can also be used on either the push or pull stroke. If you are cutting a workpiece that is face down, mount the blade with the teeth facing the handle and cut

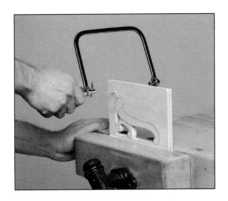

The detachable blade of a coping saw is thin enough to follow the most intricate curve.

on the pull stroke. If the workpiece is clamped end-up, install the blade with the teeth facing away from the handle and cut on the push stroke.

Japanese saws are particularly well suited to many kinds of intricate cuts. The main benefit of the double-edged ryoba saw for cutting a notch, for example, is that the same tool can be used to make the crosscut and the rip cut *(page 47)*. Because they cut on the pull stroke, Japanese saw blades can be exceptionally thin and light, so they slice through wood very quickly. Many Western woodworkers keep one or more in their tool chests because the Oriental tools sometimes are convenient to use in situations where a Western-style saw might prove clumsy.

MAKING A FLUSH CUT

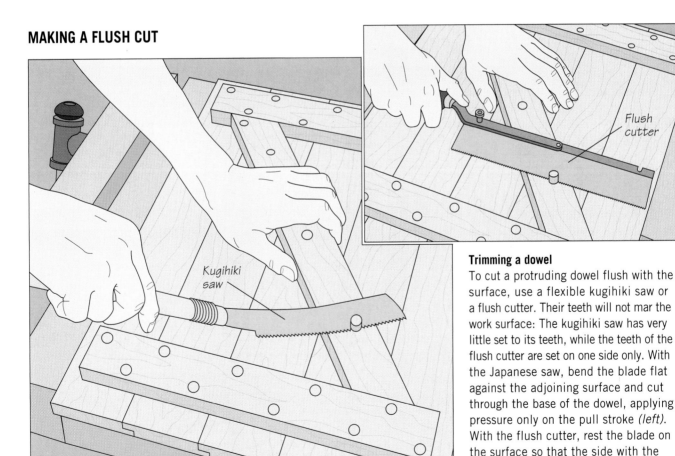

Kugihiki saw

Flush cutter

Trimming a dowel
To cut a protruding dowel flush with the surface, use a flexible kugihiki saw or a flush cutter. Their teeth will not mar the work surface: The kugihiki saw has very little set to its teeth, while the teeth of the flush cutter are set on one side only. With the Japanese saw, bend the blade flat against the adjoining surface and cut through the base of the dowel, applying pressure only on the pull stroke *(left)*. With the flush cutter, rest the blade on the surface so that the side with the set teeth is facing up, and butt the teeth against the dowel. Saw through the pin, using force on the push stroke *(above)*.

MAKING INTERIOR CUTS

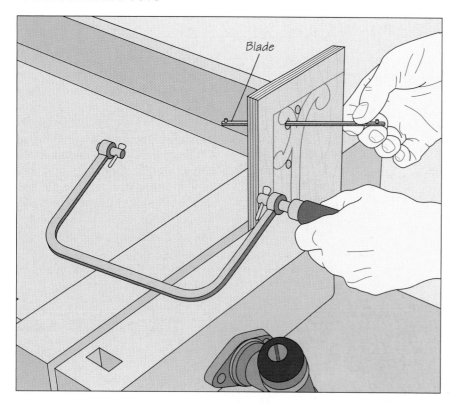

Blade

1 Setting up a coping saw
To make a curved interior cut, secure the workpiece in a vise and bore at least one hole through each waste section with a drill. The diameter of the holes should be slightly larger than the width of the saw blade. Remove the blade from the saw and insert one end through a hole in the workpiece *(left)*. Attach the blade to the frame, making sure the teeth are pointing away from the handle. Adjust the blade tension by turning the handle: clockwise to increase tension, counter-clockwise to decrease it.

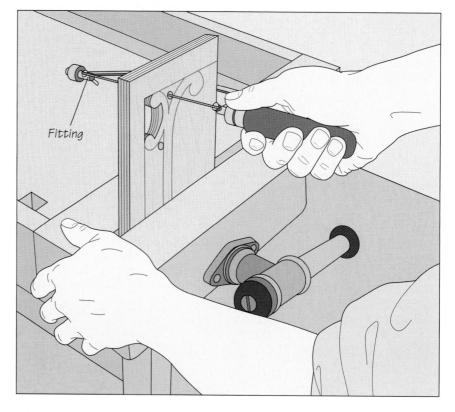

Fitting

2 Cutting the curves
Saw to one of the cutting lines, then follow the marks, continuing until you reach your starting point and the waste piece falls away. Use smooth and gentle strokes, biting into the wood when pushing the saw forward. Once the first cut is completed, remove the blade from the saw and cut away the remaining waste pieces the same way *(right)*. To align the blade teeth for tight curves, rotate the blade in the frame by turning the fittings at either end of the frame.

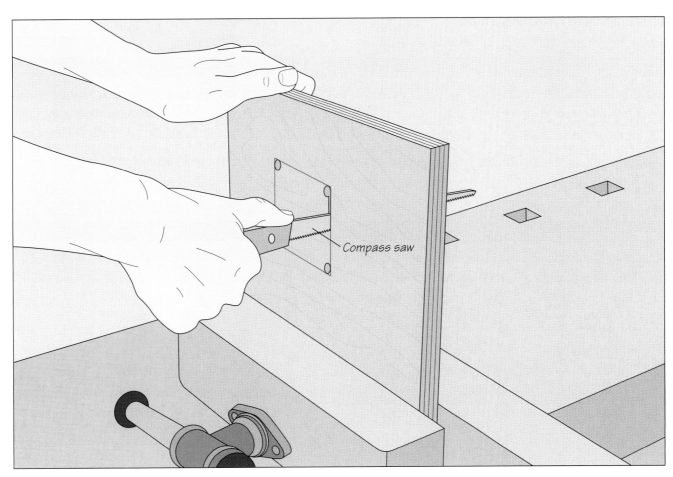

Compass saw

Making a rectangular pocket cut
Make a square-edged interior cut using a compass saw. Secure the workpiece in a vise and bore a hole at each corner of the waste section wide enough to accommodate the tip of the blade. Saw along the marked outline with slow and steady strokes. If necessary, clean up the corners with a chisel.

SHOP TIP

A V-block for curved cuts
Use a V-block to eliminate rattling and chatter when cutting tight curves in thin stock with a coping saw. Cut a V-shaped notch in a piece of plywood, then clamp the block to a work surface with the V extending off the table. Hold the workpiece flat on the block as you saw, shifting its position to center the cutting line in the V section. Be sure to install the blade with the teeth pointing toward the handle, enabling the saw to cut on the downstroke.

CUTTING CURVES IN THICK STOCK

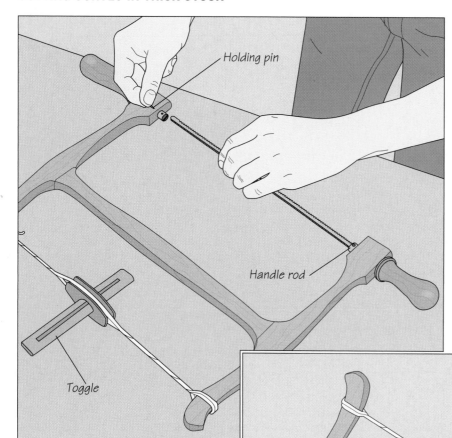

Holding pin

Handle rod

Toggle

Stretcher rail

1 Installing the bowsaw blade
To cut curves in thicker stock with a bowsaw, install your narrowest blade. Unwind the toggle to loosen the tourniquet, then insert the blade into the rods on the handles. To secure the blade, fit the holding pins through it and the handle rods *(left)*.

2 Tensioning the blade
Wind the toggle to tighten the tourniquet; this will narrow the top part of the frame and widen the bottom, increasing tension on the blade *(right)*. Once the blade is taut, rest the toggle on the rail to keep the tourniquet from unwinding. Align the teeth of the blade with the rail by turning the handles.

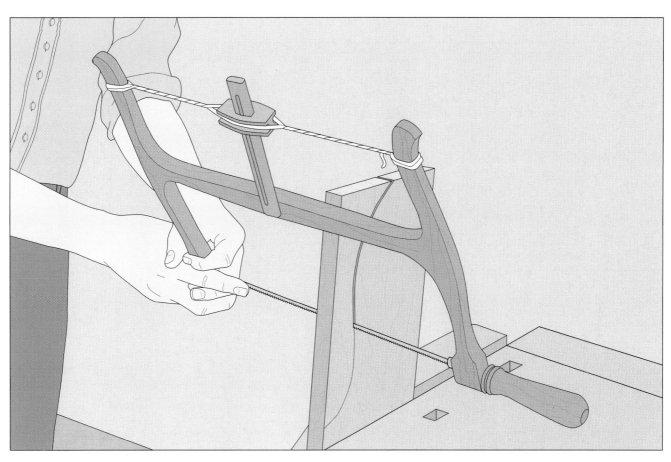

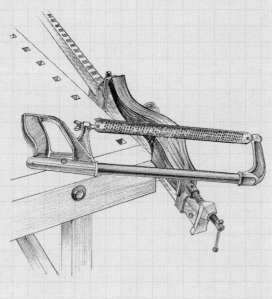

SHOP TIP

Smoothing wood with a hacksaw
Primarily a metal-cutting tool, a hacksaw can be fitted with interchangeable blades, rasps, and rifflers for rough removal of stock and for smoothing wood. To shape a contoured surface, attach the specially designed rasp to the frame of the saw as you would a standard hacksaw blade.

3 Following a curved cutting line
Grip one of the handles with both hands so that the teeth are pointing away from you. Use your right hand to hold the handle; rest your index finger on the side of the blade. Wrap the thumb and index finger of your left hand around the base of the frame and rest the remaining fingers on your right hand. Start the cut slowly with a few smooth back-and-forth strokes. Once the kerf is deep enough to hold the blade, continue sawing more firmly, applying extra pressure on the push strokes *(above)*. To follow the curved portions of the cutting line, rotate the handle to steer the saw in the desired direction.

MAKING A COPED CUT

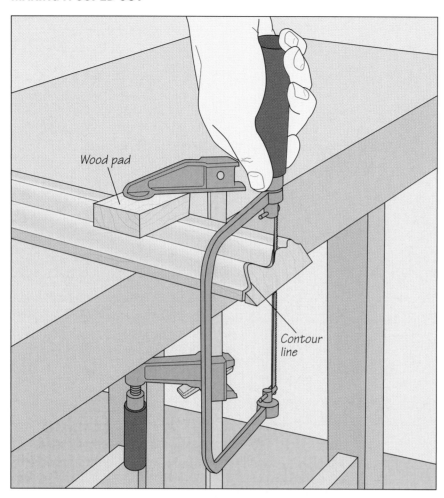

1 Coping contoured molding
Rather than using 45° mitered corners to fit molding, use a coped cut to make a precise joint. First cut the end of the molding at a 45° angle with a backsaw and miter box *(page 39)*; this will reveal a contour line on the face of the molding that you can follow with a coping saw. To make the coped cut, clamp the molding face-up on a work table, protecting the workpiece with a wood pad. Install a narrow blade on the coping saw, making sure that the teeth are facing the handle. Cut along the contour line carefully with the saw blade held perfectly upright *(left)*, biting into the wood on the upstroke. If the blade binds in the kerf, make occasional release cuts into the end grain of the waste to let small pieces fall away.

Wood pad

Contour line

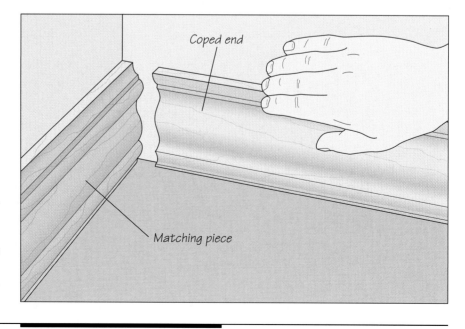

Coped end

Matching piece

2 Fitting the coped molding in place
Position the coped end against the face of the matching piece *(right)*; the fit should be perfect. Reshape any slight irregularities with a round file or fine sandpaper wrapped around a dowel. For the baseboard molding shown, fix the pieces to the wall with finishing nails. Set the nail heads below the surface using a nail set, then conceal them by rubbing the indentations with a wax stick.

USING A JAPANESE COMBINATION SAW

1 Making a crosscut

A combination saw such as a ryoba can both rip and crosscut—ideal if you are performing a task such as cutting a notch. To make the cut, secure your workpiece edge-up in a vise and butt the saw's crosscut teeth against the cutting line. Saw slowly at first, then continue with firmer strokes using the full length of the saw *(right)*. Exert more pressure on the pull stroke and keep the blade upright throughout the operation. Do not allow the rip teeth on the other side of the blade to enter the kerf; their wider set would cause the blade to bind. If the cut is deeper than the width of the saw, make an occasional rip cut to remove the waste piece before continuing with the crosscut.

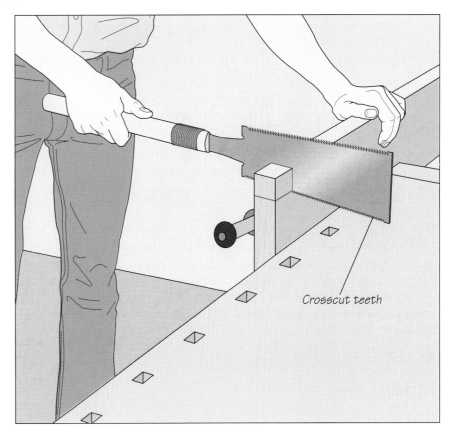

Crosscut teeth

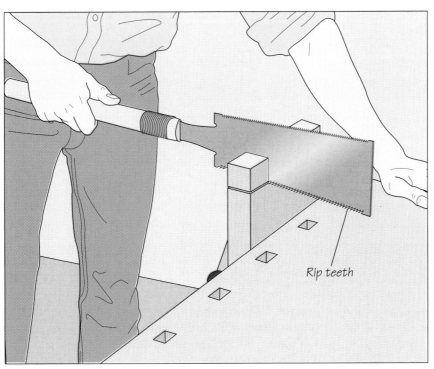

Rip teeth

2 Making a rip cut

Reposition the workpiece end-up in the vise. Cut along your marked line the same way you made the crosscut, but this time use the saw's rip teeth.

HANDSAW JOINERY

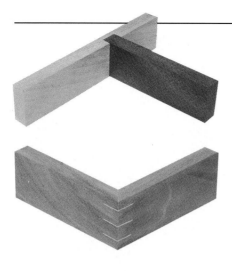

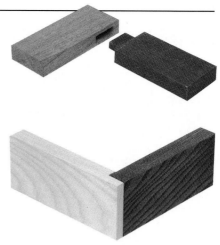

Five joints cut with handsaws: (clockwise from bottom left) a miter-and-spline, a dado, a through dovetail, a four-shouldered mortise-and-tenon, and a rabbet.

M any woodworkers instinctively turn to power tools to cut most of their joints. And while it is true that, equipped with the proper jig, a router or a table saw can churn out joints by the dozen with unrivaled efficiency, hand tools offer their own advantages. Sometimes the set-up time required by a power tool is excessive. For example, the dovetails for a single drawer can probably be cut more quickly with a handsaw and chisel than a router and a dovetail jig.

Cutting joints by hand offers another reward—the satisfaction of working closely with wood. The whir of an electric motor and a spinning blade or bit can distance you from your work. At worst, you may notice an error only after a tool has destroyed a workpiece. With a handsaw, you can cut out a joint at your own pace, controlling the blade's path with a precision equal to what any power tool can provide.

CUTTING A TENON

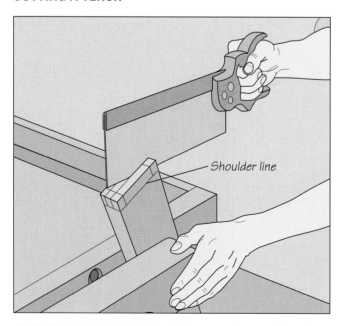

Shoulder line

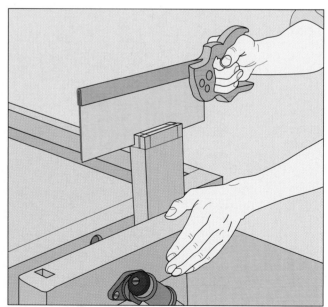

1 Cutting the cheeks
Make a tenon by cutting the cheeks first, and then the shoulders. Secure your workpiece in a vise with the end tilted forward. Cut along the lines on the end of the board with a backsaw until you reach the shoulder line of the tenon *(above, left)*;

reposition the workpiece in the vise, with the end tilted toward you, and repeat. Then, with the workpiece upright in the vise, cut down to the shoulder line, keeping the saw level throughout the operation *(above, right)*.

2 Sawing the shoulders

To remove the waste from the tenon cheeks, clamp the workpiece in a miter box with the shoulder mark aligned with the 90° slot. Cut along the shoulder line on the face of the stock *(right)*; turn the workpiece over and repeat the operation on the other side.

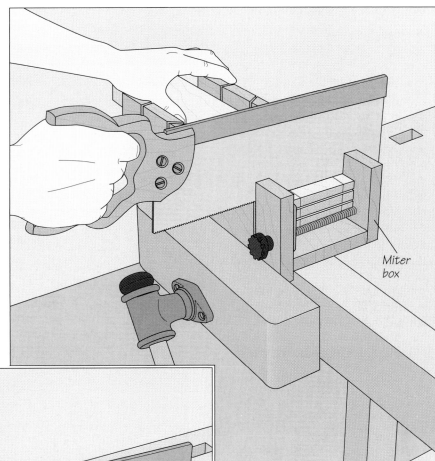

Miter box

3 Cutting away the waste on the edges of the tenon

To complete the tenon, secure the workpiece upright in the vise and cut the sides of the tenon, stopping at the shoulder line. Then, with the piece edge-up in the vise, saw along the shoulder line on the edge of the stock to the tenon. Finally, turn the board over in the vise and repeat to saw away the waste on the other edge of the tenon *(left)*.

CUTTING A THROUGH DOVETAIL

1 Marking the pins

Outline the pins for the joint, as shown in the diagram below. Mark the outside face of each workpiece with a big X, then set a cutting gauge to the thickness of the stock and scribe a line along the ends of both boards to mark the shoulder of the pins and tails. Next use a dovetail square to outline the pins on the end of one board. Start with half-pins at each edge, making sure that the narrow ends of the pins are on the outside face of the board. Mark the waste sections adjacent to the half-pins, then draw the center of the board end. Outline a pin at the center line, then mark the remainder of the pins in between *(right)*, spacing them evenly. Use a combination square to extend the pin marks to the shoulder lines.

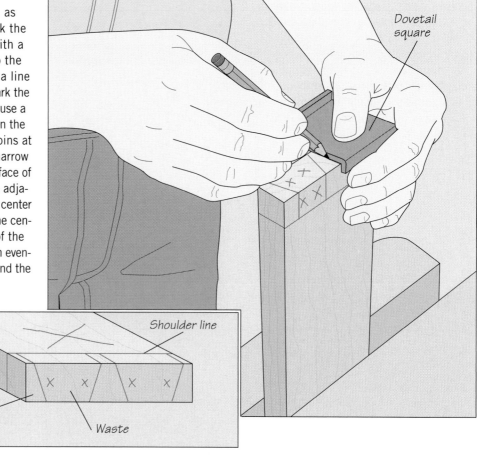

Dovetail square

Shoulder line

Half-pin

Waste

2 Cutting the pins

Secure the pin board in a vise with its outside face toward you. Use a dovetail saw to cut along the edges of the pins, working from one side of the board to the other. (Some woodworkers cut the left-hand edges first, then move on to the right-hand edges.) For each cut, align the saw blade just to the waste side of the cutting line. Use smooth, even strokes, allowing the saw to cut on the push stroke *(right)*. Continue sawing to the shoulder line, making sure that the blade is perpendicular to the line.

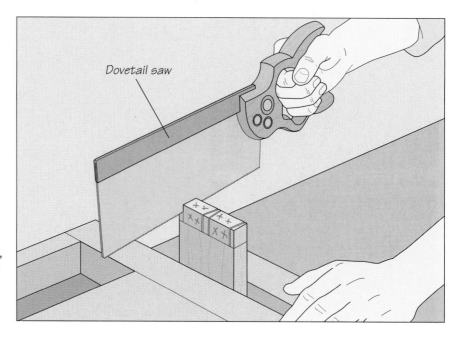

Dovetail saw

3 Removing the waste

Use a coping saw to cut away the waste wood between the pins. Slide the saw's blade into the kerf at the side of each pin and rotate the frame until it is almost level with the end of the board. Cut out as much of the waste as you can while keeping the blade about $1/16$ inch above the shoulder line *(right)*. Pare away the remaining waste with a chisel *(page 69)*.

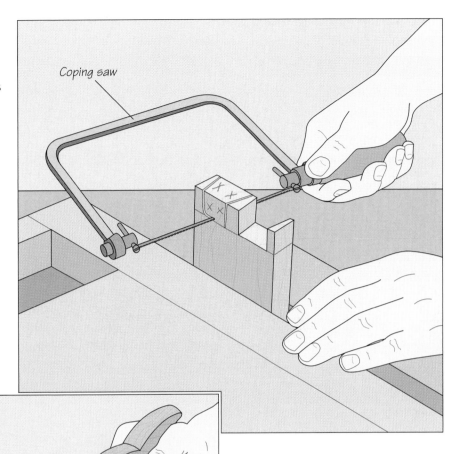

Coping saw

4 Marking and cutting the tails

Set the tail board outside-face down on the work surface. Then, hold the pin board end-down on the tail board with its outside face away from the tail board. Align the pins with the end of the tail board. Use a marking knife to outline the tails and a combination square to extend the lines onto the end of the board. Cut the tails with a dovetail saw the same way you cut the pins. Some woodworkers prefer angling the board *(left)*, rather than the saw, so that the cuts are vertical. In either case, saw smoothly and evenly, stopping just a fraction of an inch before you reach the shoulder line. Remove the bulk of the waste with a coping saw, then pare away the final bits of waste with a chisel.

Tail board

CUTTING A MITER-AND-SPLINE JOINT

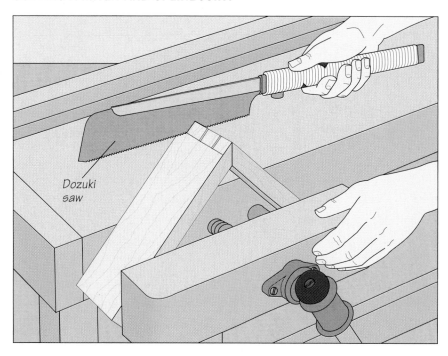

Dozuki saw

1 Cutting the grooves

Cut bevels at the ends of the boards to be joined and glue up the corner, then secure the workpiece in a vise as shown. Scribe a line along the outside faces of both boards with a cutting gauge to mark the depth of the splines, which should be slightly less than the thickness of the joint. Use a dozuki saw to cut grooves into the joint for the splines, spacing the cuts about 1 inch apart. (A backsaw will also work well, but its wider kerf means that you will have to cut thicker splines.) Saw smoothly and evenly, allowing the blade to cut on the pull stroke. Continue to the spline depth line, making sure that the blade is perpendicular *(left)*.

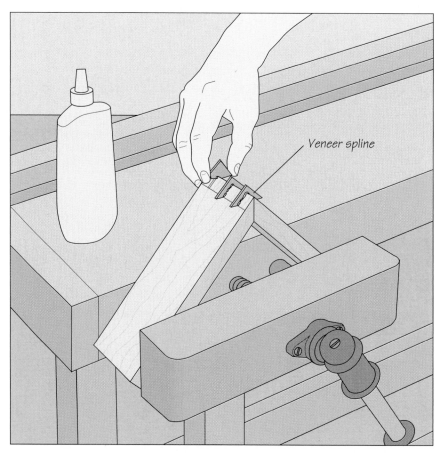

Veneer spline

2 Fitting in the splines

Cut triangular-shaped splines from veneer to fit in the grooves. For maximum strength, make sure that the grain of the splines runs along their long edge. Spread a little glue in the grooves and insert the splines long-edge down into the cuts *(right)*. The wooden wafers will absorb some of the adhesive and swell, making a solid joint. Once the glue has dried, cut and sand the projections flush with the boards.

CUTTING DADOES

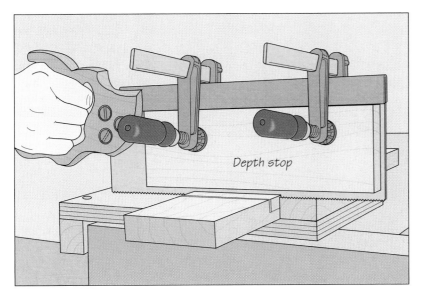

Depth stop

Cutting kerfs inside the dado outline

Mark the width of the dado on the face of the stock, then set the board on a bench hook *(page 37)*. To ensure that all the kerfs are cut to the correct depth, clamp a depth stop on one side of a backsaw blade. The depth stop should be as wide as the blade from the teeth to the bottom of the spine, less the desired depth of the dado. Saw into the workpiece at one of the width marks to cut an edge of the dado, stopping when the depth stop is flush against the face of the stock. Repeat to cut the channel's other edge *(left)*. To remove as much waste as possible, saw a number of kerfs between the two cuts, working at roughly $1/8$-inch intervals. Remove the remaining waste with a chisel.

SAWING RABBETS

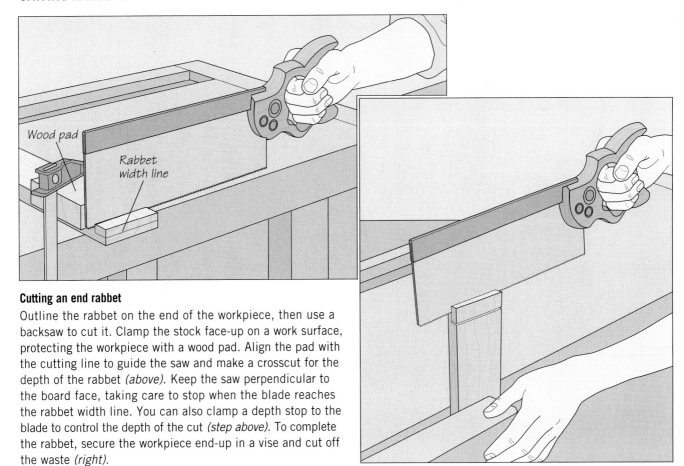

Wood pad

Rabbet
width line

Cutting an end rabbet

Outline the rabbet on the end of the workpiece, then use a backsaw to cut it. Clamp the stock face-up on a work surface, protecting the workpiece with a wood pad. Align the pad with the cutting line to guide the saw and make a crosscut for the depth of the rabbet *(above)*. Keep the saw perpendicular to the board face, taking care to stop when the blade reaches the rabbet width line. You can also clamp a depth stop to the blade to control the depth of the cut *(step above)*. To complete the rabbet, secure the workpiece end-up in a vise and cut off the waste *(right)*.

CHISELS AND BORING TOOLS

The wood chisel is one of woodworking's indispensable tools. This is no wonder: Although saws, drills, planes, and other tools have been motorized successfully, no suitable substitute has been found for the simple—and versatile—wood chisel. Strong enough to withstand the forceful blows of a mallet and hog out great quantities of waste wood, the ordinary chisel is also light and well-balanced, so that sensitive hands can use it to impart the most precise shapes.

When the table saw is turned off and the whine of router and drill ceases, the chisel is put to work squaring corners, trimming tenons, smoothing curves, and trueing dovetails. The varieties of chisels and some of the techniques for using them for a number of woodworking tasks are explained in the following pages.

The results you obtain at the workbench will be strongly influenced by the quality of your chisels and the keenness of their blades. Time invested in learning and using sharpening skills *(page 65)* will help produce superior work. Invest also in good-quality tools. Naturally, strength is one requirement. The steel must also take and maintain a sharp edge; the handle must withstand

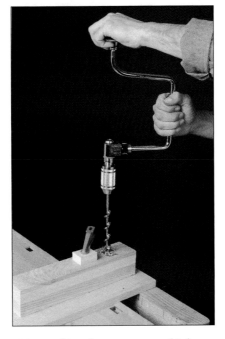

Mounted in a brace, an auger bit bores a hole through a block of hardwood. Aligning the bit over the gap between the workbench and the vise permits the hole to be drilled without marring the bench top.

hard use; the entire tool must be well balanced—easy to hold and easy to guide. When shopping for a chisel, discuss your needs with dealers and other woodworkers. Look for high-quality steel, a well-fitted handle, and a blade that is finely finished top and bottom. Also check that the back of the chisel blade is perfectly flat, particularly just behind the cutting edge. A flat back is essential when you are using the chisel for paring, as it provides an even bearing surface that increases accuracy. An old chisel may be pitted with rust, but it can still give adequate service once it has been reground.

Electric motors now power the drills and other boring devices in most workshops. Nevertheless, most woodworkers still keep a brace, hand drill, and push drill handy, for these hand tools have unique abilities not readily duplicated by power tools, especially working in tight quarters or when precise control of a hole's depth is required. Some of the tools and their uses are detailed starting on page 70.

Although new hand tools sometimes cost as much as their electric counterparts, good used hand tools are more affordable. They deserve a place in every well-equipped tool chest.

A paring chisel shaves away a sliver of waste from one side of a dovetail. The skew chisels on the workbench are used to trim waste to the shoulder line.

A COLLECTION OF CHISELS

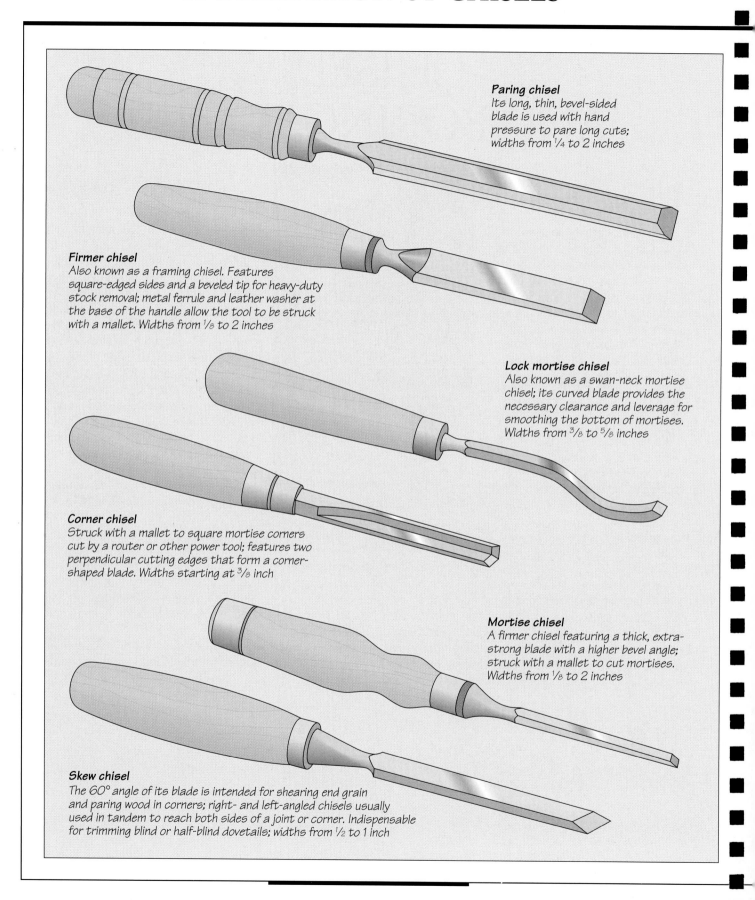

Paring chisel
Its long, thin, bevel-sided blade is used with hand pressure to pare long cuts; widths from 1/4 to 2 inches

Firmer chisel
Also known as a framing chisel. Features square-edged sides and a beveled tip for heavy-duty stock removal; metal ferrule and leather washer at the base of the handle allow the tool to be struck with a mallet. Widths from 1/8 to 2 inches

Lock mortise chisel
Also known as a swan-neck mortise chisel; its curved blade provides the necessary clearance and leverage for smoothing the bottom of mortises. Widths from 3/8 to 5/8 inches

Corner chisel
Struck with a mallet to square mortise corners cut by a router or other power tool; features two perpendicular cutting edges that form a corner-shaped blade. Widths starting at 3/8 inch

Mortise chisel
A firmer chisel featuring a thick, extra-strong blade with a higher bevel angle; struck with a mallet to cut mortises. Widths from 1/8 to 2 inches

Skew chisel
The 60° angle of its blade is intended for shearing end grain and paring wood in corners; right- and left-angled chisels usually used in tandem to reach both sides of a joint or corner. Indispensable for trimming blind or half-blind dovetails; widths from 1/2 to 1 inch

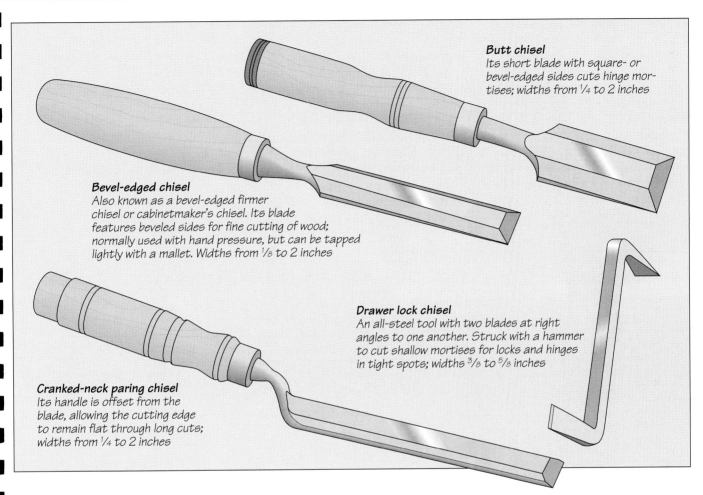

Butt chisel
Its short blade with square- or bevel-edged sides cuts hinge mortises; widths from 1/4 to 2 inches

Bevel-edged chisel
Also known as a bevel-edged firmer chisel or cabinetmaker's chisel. Its blade features beveled sides for fine cutting of wood; normally used with hand pressure, but can be tapped lightly with a mallet. Widths from 1/8 to 2 inches

Drawer lock chisel
An all-steel tool with two blades at right angles to one another. Struck with a hammer to cut shallow mortises for locks and hinges in tight spots; widths 3/8 to 5/8 inches

Cranked-neck paring chisel
Its handle is offset from the blade, allowing the cutting edge to remain flat through long cuts; widths from 1/4 to 2 inches

STORING CHISELS

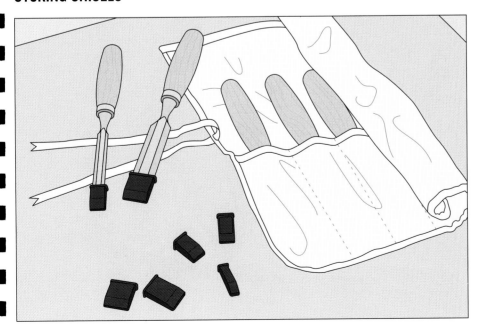

Protecting chisels from damage
The cutting edges of chisels can be nicked if they are stored loosely in a toolbox or on a workbench. Protect your chisels with plastic guards or a tool roll. Chisel guards are available in a variety of widths to fit any tip size, and can usually be bought either individually or in sets of five or ten. Tool rolls are generally made from leather or heavy-duty canvas or cloth, with anywhere from six to 12 slots for chisel blades and a flap that folds over the handles.

ANATOMY OF A CHISEL

A chisel blade is attached to its handle in one of two ways. The more common style features a narrow metal tang that is driven into a wooden handle or molded into a plastic one. A different construction features a hollow socket that holds the handle.

The blade itself may be straight-sided or beveled on its upper face. While reducing the tool's strength, the bevel enables the cutting edge to get into corners and restricted spaces. Because bevel-edged chisels are comfortable to use with hand pressure, they rank among the cabinetmaker's favorite hand tools.

Chisels fall into three basic categories depending on the blade type. Firmer chisels are durable tools that can be struck with a mallet. They have heavy bolsters, necks, and cutting edges, along with tough handles supported by a metal ferrule. Some models include leather washers, one just below the ferrule and another on the head of the handle, to cushion the impact of mallet blows.

Mortise chisels are like firmer chisels but with thicker blades. The handles usually feature a ferrule at both the top and the bottom.

Finally, there are paring chisels, relatively delicate tools with long, thin, beveled blades, and fine wooden handles not meant to be struck with mallets.

Woods like ebony, rosewood, and hickory were once used for chisel handles, but have been replaced mostly by beech and boxwood.

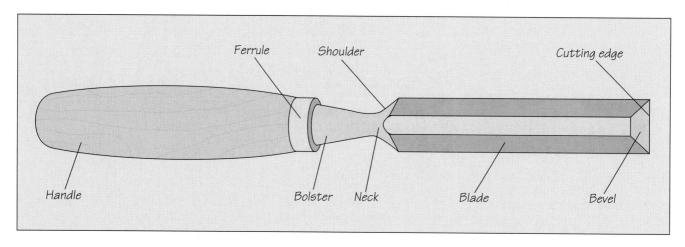

Japanese bevel-edged chisels have earned a reputation as the world's finest chisels. They often feature red oak handles; the bottom face of the laminated steel blades is usually slightly concave to reduce friction and facilitate sharpening. Although Japanese chisels are about the same length overall as Western-style tools, their chisel blades are shorter, with longer shoulders and tangs.

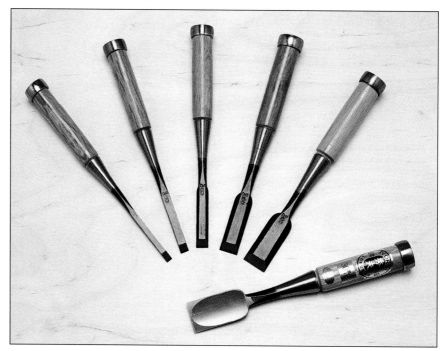

BASIC CHISELING

Although the chisel, like other hand tools, is a relatively safe instrument, its sharp edge can inflict serious injury—or destroy a workpiece—unless its user adopts a few simple techniques. Always maintain a balanced, stable posture when cutting; that way, a slip will not lead to an uncontrolled cut. Always clamp your workpiece, and keep both hands behind the cutting edge.

When paring thin slivers of wood, use both hands: one on the tool handle to exert pressure and the other on the blade to guide the cut. As shown in the photo at right, butting your blade-hand against the edge of the workpiece enables you to push with as much force as necessary without exposing the hand to the cutting edge of the blade.

When you strike a chisel with a mallet, hold both tools firmly, taking care to grip the chisel down from the end of the handle. In general, use a mallet with a chisel to cut away large amounts of waste wood; paring is usually sufficient for trimming or cleaning up saw cuts.

As the following pages illustrate, the angle at which you hold a chisel determines the kind of cut you will make. For aggressive removal of waste, hold the blade perpendicular to the surface. Paring, on the other hand, works best with the blade parallel to the surface; try to shear away waste in thin shavings rather than with one mighty cut. Whatever angle you choose, always pare with the grain of the wood. Working against the grain can make it difficult to cut in a straight line; the blade will tend to dive into the wood, resulting in split wood fibers and rough edges.

Chisels are usually used with the beveled face up. However, certain operations may produce better results with the blade bevel-down. In some cases, working with the bevel down will prevent the cutting edge from digging into the wood.

A few safety reminders: Use only sharp chisels. A tool with a well-honed blade can slice through wood with ease; a dull blade forces you to exert too much pressure—a recipe for error and injury. Always work with the blade cutting away from you.

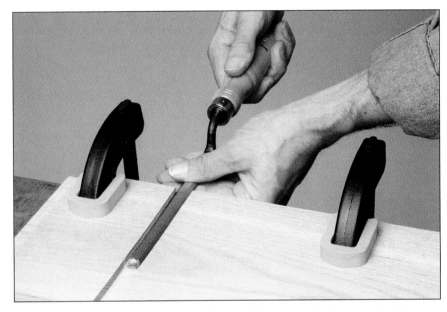

The crank-necked paring chisel is the ideal tool for cutting the bottom of a dado to a uniform depth. The tool's offset handle allows the blade to remain flat throughout the operation—even when the length of the cut exceeds the length of the blade.

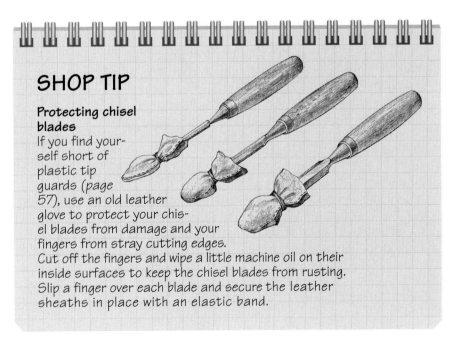

SHOP TIP

Protecting chisel blades
If you find yourself short of plastic tip guards (page 57), use an old leather glove to protect your chisel blades from damage and your fingers from stray cutting edges. Cut off the fingers and wipe a little machine oil on their inside surfaces to keep the chisel blades from rusting. Slip a finger over each blade and secure the leather sheaths in place with an elastic band.

CUTTING A NOTCH

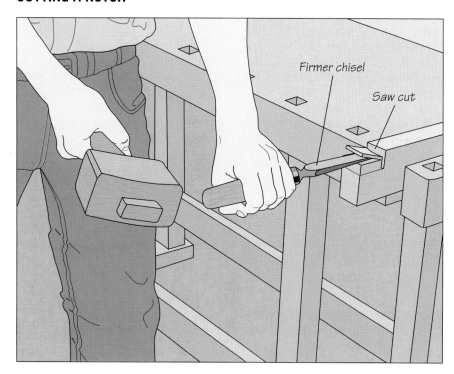

Firmer chisel

Saw cut

1 Removing the waste
Secure the workpiece edge-up in a vise and saw a kerf into the edge of the stock to define the end of the notch. Stop the kerf at the cutting line on the face of the board; the kerf will sever the wood fibers at the end of the notch, making it possible to shear away the waste with a chisel without splintering the wood. Using a firmer chisel about as wide as the thickness of the workpiece, butt the tip of the blade against the end of the board about $\frac{1}{8}$ inch below the top edge. Hold the blade bevel-up and parallel to the edge of the workpiece and strike the handle firmly with a wooden mallet *(left)*, cutting off a thin layer of waste to the saw kerf. Continue slicing away the waste in this fashion until you are about $\frac{1}{8}$ inch above the cutting line on the board face.

2 Final paring
With the workpiece still in the vise, shave away the remaining waste with the firmer chisel or a paring chisel. Press the flat side of the blade against the bottom of the notch, holding the chisel handle with your right hand and the blade between the thumb and fingers of your left hand. Rest the index finger of your left hand against the end of the workpiece to protect the hand from the tip of the blade. Push the chisel toward the saw kerf *(right)*, shaving away the last slivers of waste to the cutting line. If the blade catches on the wood fibers, ease the cutting edge through the wood by moving the handle from side to side while applying forward pressure.

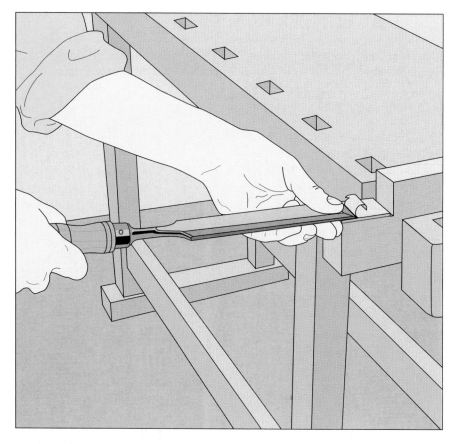

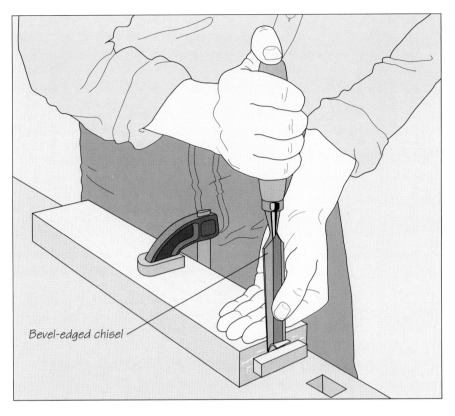

Bevel-edged chisel

Vertical paring

To shave away waste from a vertical surface, such as the shoulders of a tenon, clamp the workpiece to a work surface. Holding the handle of a bevel-edged chisel with your right hand, use the thumb of your left hand to butt the flat side of the blade against the tenon shoulder. Rest the fingers of your left hand on the face of the board. Leaning over the workpiece and keeping your arms locked in position, slice away thin slivers of waste at a time *(left)*, exerting pressure by moving your upper body rather than your arms or hands. Once you reach the cutting line, turn the workpiece over and repeat on the other side of the tenon.

BUILD IT YOURSELF

A WALL-MOUNTED CHISEL RACK

Keep your chisels organized and in full view in a shop-made wall rack. Build the rack from three strips: the back piece should be longer than the others so its ends can be screwed to the wall; make the middle piece twice as wide as the outside pieces.

Cut slots for your chisels along the edges of the middle piece. The slots should be about ½ inch deep and slightly wider than your chisel blades. Glue the three pieces together and mount the rack on a wall as you would a screwdriver rack *(page 121)*.

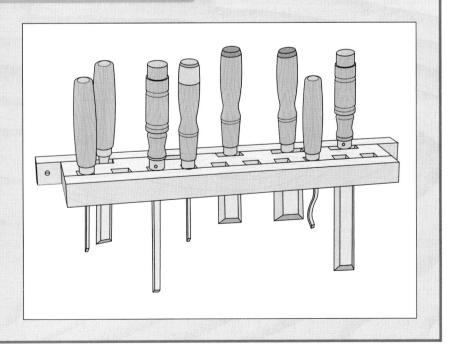

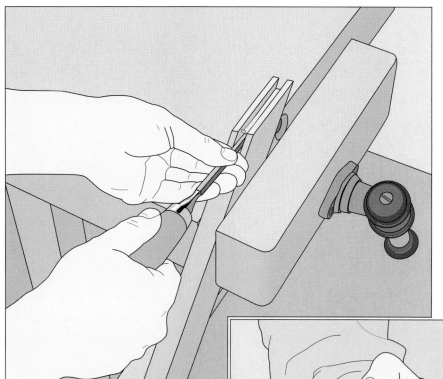

Paring a groove
Secure the workpiece in a vise. The illustration shows a piece for a miter-and-spline joint, with saw cuts already made defining the groove. With the mitered end up, angle the board to position the groove level with the work surface. Using a bevel-edged chisel slightly narrower than the groove, work with the grain, shaving away waste in thin layers as you would in paring a notch *(page 60)*. Clean out the groove periodically so the shavings will not cover the blade and obscure the cutting edge.

Support board

Shaping a circular edge
To smooth a curved cut, clamp the workpiece face up to a work surface. To protect the bench, clamp a support board between the stock and the work surface. Using a bevel-edged chisel, grip the tool as you would for vertical paring *(page 61)*, slicing away thin layers of waste along the edges of the cut *(right)*. Push the tool using a side-to-side rocking motion.

CUTTING A DOOR HINGE MORTISE

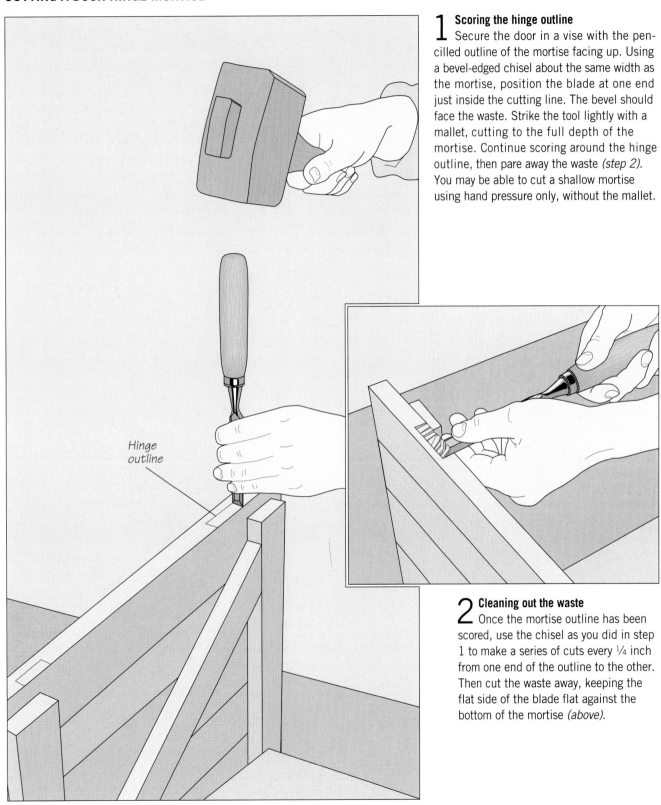

Hinge
outline

1 Scoring the hinge outline
Secure the door in a vise with the pencilled outline of the mortise facing up. Using a bevel-edged chisel about the same width as the mortise, position the blade at one end just inside the cutting line. The bevel should face the waste. Strike the tool lightly with a mallet, cutting to the full depth of the mortise. Continue scoring around the hinge outline, then pare away the waste *(step 2)*. You may be able to cut a shallow mortise using hand pressure only, without the mallet.

2 Cleaning out the waste
Once the mortise outline has been scored, use the chisel as you did in step 1 to make a series of cuts every ¼ inch from one end of the outline to the other. Then cut the waste away, keeping the flat side of the blade flat against the bottom of the mortise *(above)*.

TRIMMING IN RESTRICTED SPACES

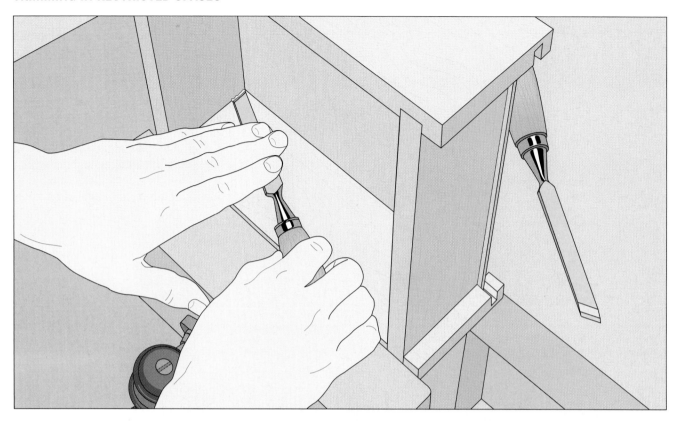

Cleaning up a corner

Use a skew chisel to trim a surface in a tight spot that a standard chisel is unable to reach, such as the inside corner of a drawer. Secure the drawer in a vise and hold the chisel in the drawer bevel up, pressing the blade flat and guiding it with your left hand. Push the chisel toward the corner lightly to trim the surface *(above)*.

SHOP TIP

A makeshift router plane
If you need to smooth the bottom of a dado, but do not own a router plane, you can improvise a tool that does the same job. Mount a firmer chisel bevel down in a sharpening guide, with the microbevel *(page 65)* flat on the bottom of the dado. Butt a support board the same thickness as your workpiece against the dado to keep your makeshift plane level. Then advance the chisel along the channel. Pushing it slowly will prevent the cutting edge from gouging the bottom of the dado.

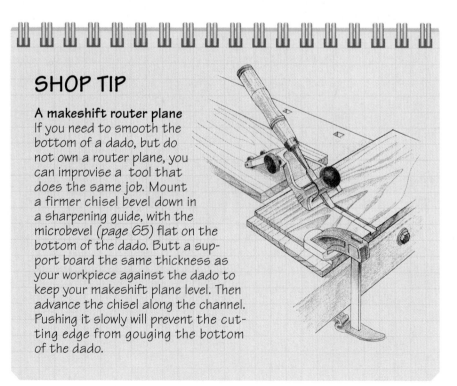

SHARPENING A CHISEL

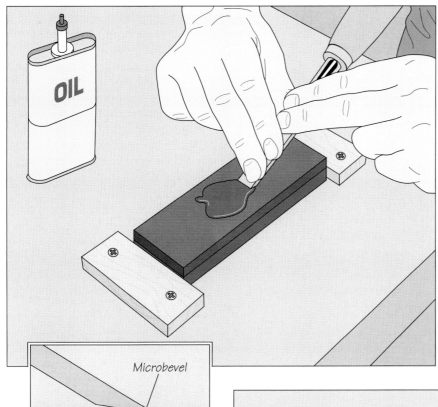

1 Honing the cutting edge
Sharpening a chisel blade involves two steps: honing a secondary bevel on the forward edge of the existing bevel—called a microbevel—then removing the resulting burr. To form the microbevel, lay a combination stone coarse side up and nail cleats to the work surface to keep the stone from moving. Saturate the stone with the appropriate lubricant—either water or a light oil—until it pools on the surface. Start by holding the blade with the existing bevel flat on the stone; then raise it about 5° and slide the cutting edge on the stone with long, elliptical passes *(left)*. Apply moderate pressure until a microbevel forms *(inset)*. Turn the stone over to make a few passes on the fine side.

Microbevel

2 Lapping the burr
To remove the burr that forms on the flat side of the blade—a process woodworkers call "lapping" the burr—saturate the stone once again. Holding the chisel blade flat on the fine side of the stone, bevel side up, move it in a circular pattern *(right)* until the flat side of the cutting edge is smooth to the touch. A few strokes should suffice.

CHISEL JOINERY

Although modern machinery may have relegated the chisel to a back-up role in many joint-making operations, this particular hand tool remains indispensable for cutting the finishing touches on joints. Two everyday examples are cleaning out the corners of a router-cut blind dado and shaving away the last slivers of waste from dovetails cut by a saw.

A chisel is also a good choice for chopping out mortises, particularly when only a few joints are involved. For small jobs, the speed of power tools is usually offset by setup time. It is faster to hand-cut the mortises for one table, for example, than to set up a mortising attachment on a drill press.

There is no single correct sequence in chiseling a mortise. Some wood-

With its 90° angled cutting edge, a corner chisel squares the corners of a mortise cut by a router.

workers prefer to start their cuts in the middle of the mortise outline and work toward the ends. You can just as easily start at one end and proceed to the other, as shown below.

One requirement that does not vary, however, is using the correct tool for each stage of the operation. A mortise chisel will cut a cavity with cleaner edges than either a firmer or ordinary bevel-edged chisel, and a swan-neck chisel simplifies clean-up of the cavity. A corner chisel is useful for squaring mortise corners cut by a router.

The dado is another joint that can be chiseled effectively. The technique shown on page 68—shaving off the waste wood in a series of thin layers—may seem relatively time-consuming, but the resulting channel will be square and clean.

HAND-CUTTING A MORTISE

1 Chopping the mortise
Clamp your stock to a work surface. Then, starting about ⅛ inch inside the cutting line at one end of the outline, hold a mortise chisel vertically and strike it with a wooden mallet, making a cut that is about ¼ inch deep. Use a chisel the same width as the mortise and be sure that the beveled face of the blade is facing the waste. Then make another cut ¼ inch from the first *(right)* and lever out the waste *(step 2)*.

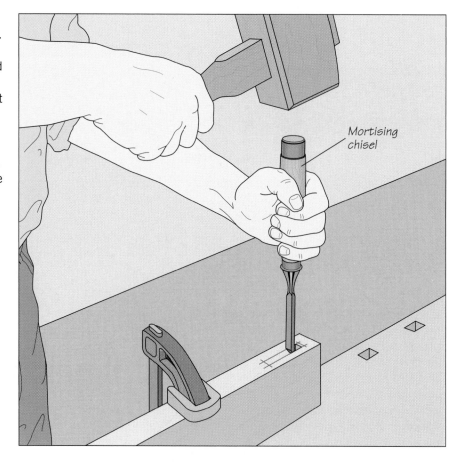

Mortising chisel

2 Levering out the waste

With the blade wedged in the cut, tilt the handle down toward the uncut portion of the outline. The tip of the blade will dig in under the waste wood and sever it from the bottom of the mortise. Continue making a cut every ¼ inch as in step 1 and levering out the waste *(right)*. When you are ⅛ inch from the other end of the outline, turn the chisel around so the bevel faces in the opposite direction. Make a cut and lever out the waste. Repeat the process until you reach the desired depth of the mortise.

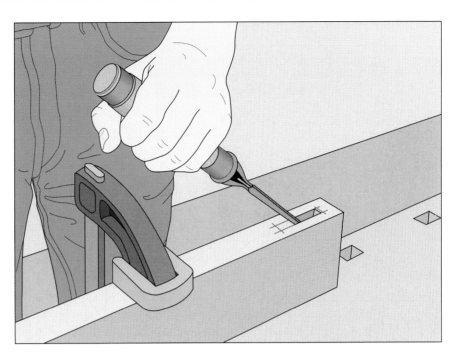

3 Smoothing the bottom and trimming the ends of the mortise

Use a lock mortise chisel—also called a swan-neck chisel—the same width as the mortise to smooth the bottom of the cavity. Holding the rounded back face of the blade against one end of the mortise, push the chisel toward the other end *(left)*. The tip of the blade will scrape along the bottom of the mortise, shaving off waste and leaving the surface smooth and even. For a long mortise, repeat from the other end. Trim the ends of the cavity with the same mortising chisel used to chop out the mortise. With a mortise chisel held vertically, pare away the ⅛-inch-wide waste sections at either end of the mortise. This time, align the chisel blade with the cutting marks at the ends of the outline and pare to the line.

Lock
mortise
chisel

CHISELING A DADO

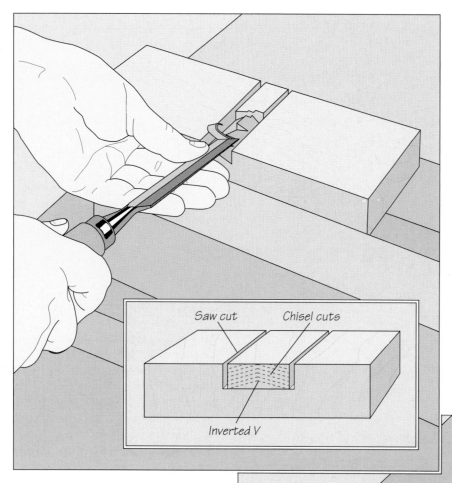

Saw cut   Chisel cuts

Inverted V

1 Chiseling the waste
Secure the workpiece in a vise and cut the edges of the dado to the desired depth with a backsaw. Then, using a bevel-edged chisel slightly narrower than the dado, remove the waste with a series of shallow cuts that leave an inverted V at the bottom of the groove *(inset)*. Angle the blade so that one side rests against one of the saw cuts and shave off thin layers of waste, stopping halfway along the channel. Angling the cuts, continue shaving away the waste in this fashion until the lower edge of the blade reaches the bottom of the dado. Remove the waste on the other side of the channel *(left)*, then turn the workpiece around and repeat to clear the waste from the other half

2 Final paring
To remove the peak left in the middle of the dado, pare away the waste with the chisel handle tilted down about 10°. Push the chisel along the channel to slice away a thin layer of waste *(right)*, stopping about halfway along the dado. Continue until you reach the the bottom of the dado, making the final pass with the chisel blade flat against the bottom. Turn the workpiece around and repeat for the other half.

FINE-TUNING A DOVETAIL JOINT

Trimming to the shoulder line

To remove the waste from dovetails cut with a handsaw, use a bevel-edged chisel slightly narrower than the space between the tails at the shoulder line. Set the tail board face down and align the tip of the chisel with the shoulder line. Using your thumb to hold the blade vertical, push the chisel straight down to pare away the final sliver of waste *(right)*. Repeat the process between the other tails until there is no waste beyond the shoulder line. To trim to the cutting lines on the sides of the tails, secure the work-piece end-out in a vise and use the bevel-edged chisel horizontally to pare away any waste. Then, with the workpiece clamped end-up, remove waste wood in the corners between the tails and the shoulder with a skew chisel. Holding the flat face of the blade flush against the shoulder, guide the tip of the blade to the base of the tail to clean up the corner *(below)*. Use the same tools and techniques on the pin board.

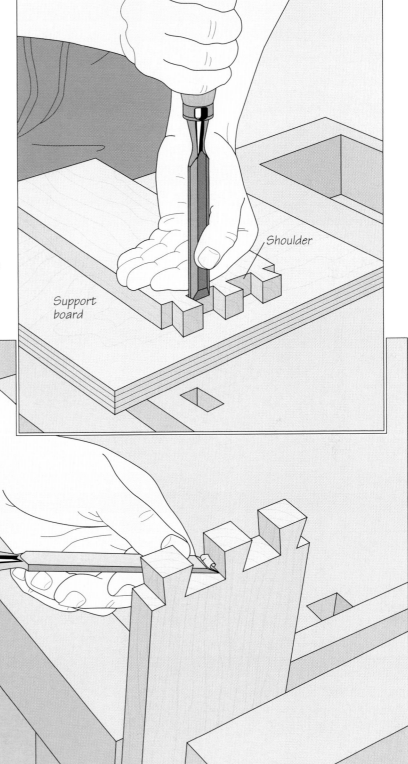

A BATTERY OF TOOLS FOR BORING

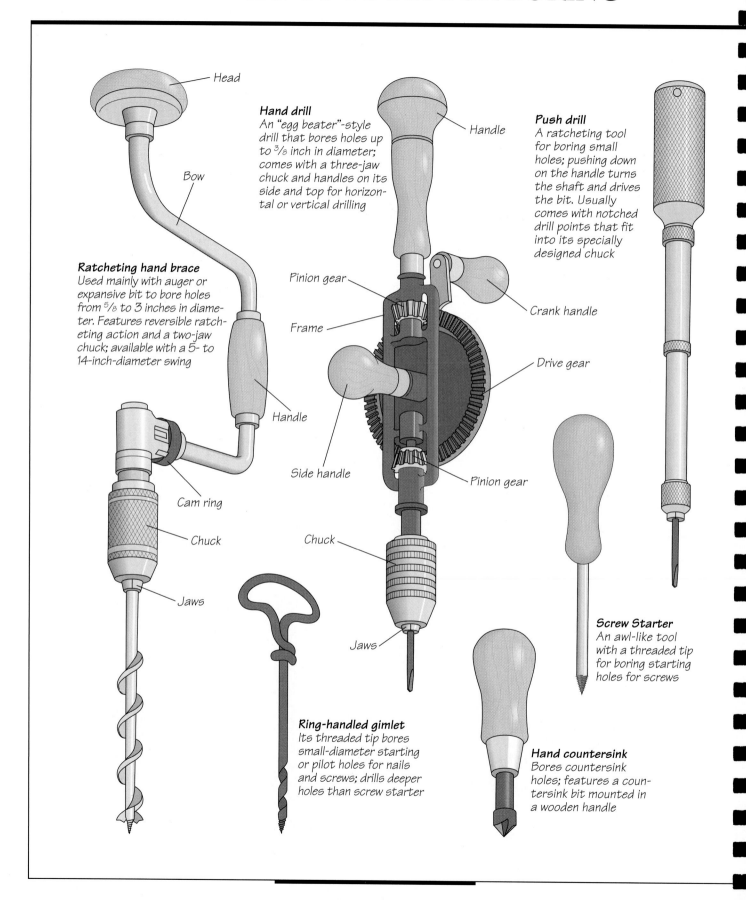

Head

Bow

Ratcheting hand brace
Used mainly with auger or expansive bit to bore holes from ⁵⁄₈ to 3 inches in diameter. Features reversible ratcheting action and a two-jaw chuck; available with a 5- to 14-inch-diameter swing

Hand drill
An "egg beater"-style drill that bores holes up to ³⁄₈ inch in diameter; comes with a three-jaw chuck and handles on its side and top for horizontal or vertical drilling

Handle

Push drill
A ratcheting tool for boring small holes; pushing down on the handle turns the shaft and drives the bit. Usually comes with notched drill points that fit into its specially designed chuck

Pinion gear

Frame

Crank handle

Drive gear

Side handle

Pinion gear

Handle

Cam ring

Chuck

Jaws

Chuck

Jaws

Screw Starter
An awl-like tool with a threaded tip for boring starting holes for screws

Ring-handled gimlet
Its threaded tip bores small-diameter starting or pilot holes for nails and screws; drills deeper holes than screw starter

Hand countersink
Bores countersink holes; features a countersink bit mounted in a wooden handle

A RANGE OF BRACE AND DRILL BITS

Double-twist auger bit
Also known as a Jennings pattern auger bit; bores holes from 1/4 to 1 1/2 inches in diameter. Features two spurs and a lead screw; the spiral throat allows waste and sawdust to pass quickly from the hole

Countersink bit
Used with hand brace or drill to bore counter-sink holes 1/2, 5/8 and 3/4 inch in diameter

Solid-center auger bit
A general-purpose brace bit for boring holes from 1/4 to 1 inch in diameter; features a lead screw and two sharpened cutting spurs. Available in a wide range of shank lengths

Spoon bit
A traditional gouge-shaped bit used in a brace to bore 3/8- to 3/4-inch holes for chair legs and dowels; also available in tapered form for reaming

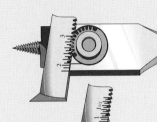

Expansive bit
An adjustable bit with two interchangeable cutters; used with a brace to bore holes from 5/8 to 3 inches in diameter

Center bit
Fits into a brace to bore shallow holes from 3/16 and 2 1/4 inches in diameter

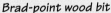

Drill point
A fluted bit used in a push or hand drill to bore holes from 1/16 to 11/64 inch in diameter

Screwdriver bit
A flat-tip bit used with a brace to drive slot-head screws; usually available in 3/8- to 3/4-inch blade widths

Twist drill
An all-purpose drill with a straight shank that only fits in three-jaw drill chucks; bores holes from 1/16 to 1/2 inch in diameter

Brad-point wood bit
Bores holes from 1/8 to 1 inch in diameter; has a short brad lead and spurs. Available with straight or tapered shank to fit in hand drill or brace

Braces come in many shapes and sizes depending on the job they are designed to perform. The close-quarter or joist brace (far right) can bore holes in tight spots that would be cramped for a conventional brace. Its lever is set at a 90° angle to the bit, enabling the tool to be cranked while the head is held directly over the hole. The short-throw brace (near right) is essentially a standard brace with a shorter swing radius—a useful feature for restricted spaces that cannot accommodate the 12-inch swing of the typical standard brace handle.

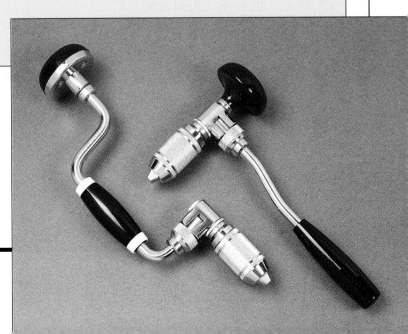

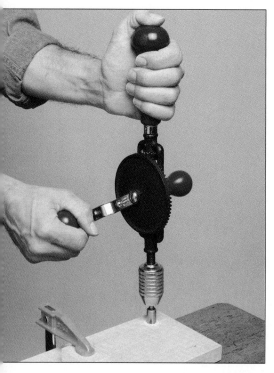

Fitted with a countersink bit, a hand drill widens the mouth of a pilot hole to allow the screw head to be set flush with the surface.

Before the electric drill and the drill press, craftsmen used braces and hand drills to bore holes in wood. Like their electric counterparts, these traditional hand tools accept a variety of bits to drill holes of different type and diameter.

Bits for braces and hand drills are not interchangeable. As shown on the previous page, brace bits feature square, tapered tangs that mate with the two-jaw chuck of a brace. The three-jaw chuck of a hand drill accepts only straight-shaft bits. Hand drills frequently come with a set of drill points, which are stored in the handle. Push drills, a type of hand drill used to bore very small holes, can only use notched drill points held in the chuck by a ball-bearing mechanism.

To bore a full range of holes you need both types of tools. As a rule of thumb, drill holes up to ¼ inch in diameter with either a push drill and drill point, or a hand drill fitted with a twist bit, drill point, or brad-point bit. The hand drill can be fitted with bits up to ½ inch in diameter. For larger holes, from ½ to 3 inches in diameter, use a brace fitted with an auger bit, expansive bit, or a center bit. Auger bits are your best choice for boring deep holes as they are easy to keep centered. The solid-center bit is the stronger of the two auger styles and is the preferred type for longer bits. Brace bits frequently have lead screws, which makes them self-starting. If you are using a bit with no lead screw, bore a small starting hole with a gimlet or a screw-starter to keep the bit from slipping.

You can use either a hand drill or brace to bore holes for screws, depending on the gauge of the screw. A common sequence is to start with a counterbore hole drilled with a brad point bit, then continue with a hand drill and drill point to bore clearance holes. The pilot hole is bored next, and a brace and screwdriver bit can then be used to drive the screw. Countersink holes can be drilled using a brace or hand drill fitted with a countersink bit, or with a hand countersink.

MAKING STARTING HOLES

Using a gimlet

Hold the workpiece steady on a flat surface and set the tip of a gimlet on the marked point for the hole. Press the gimlet into the wood and rotate it to bore a small starting hole *(right)*. Be sure to keep the tool vertical throughout the operation. To bore your hole, set the tip of a drill or brace bit in the starting hole.

BORING HOLES WITH A BRACE AND BIT

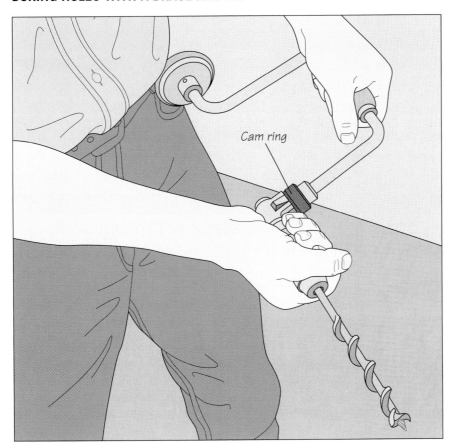

Cam ring

1 Installing a bit
Set the cam ring to the non-ratcheting position. Then, holding the chuck with one hand, crank the handle to open the jaws of the tool as wide as necessary. Insert the bit shank in the chuck, making sure that the tangs fit into the V grooves of the jaws. Crank the handle in the opposite direction; to finish tightening, steady the head of the brace against your hip and crank the handle while holding the chuck *(left)*. Adjust the cam ring to the ratcheting position and turn the chuck by hand to make sure it is tight.

SHOP TIP

Eliminating bit splintering
Boring through an unsupported workpiece often results in splintering on the opposite face. One solution is to stop boring just as the tip of the bit's lead screw emerges. Then turn the workpiece over, set the bit in the small opening pierced by the lead screw and finish drilling the hole. A back-up block clamped to the bottom of the piece will also reduce the chance of splintering.

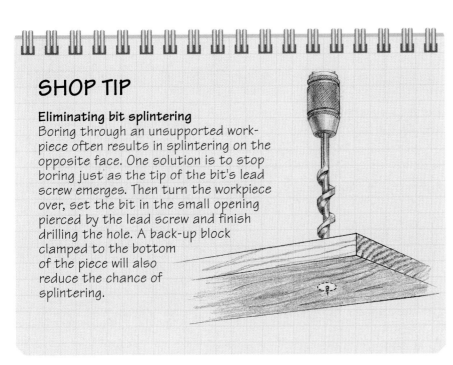

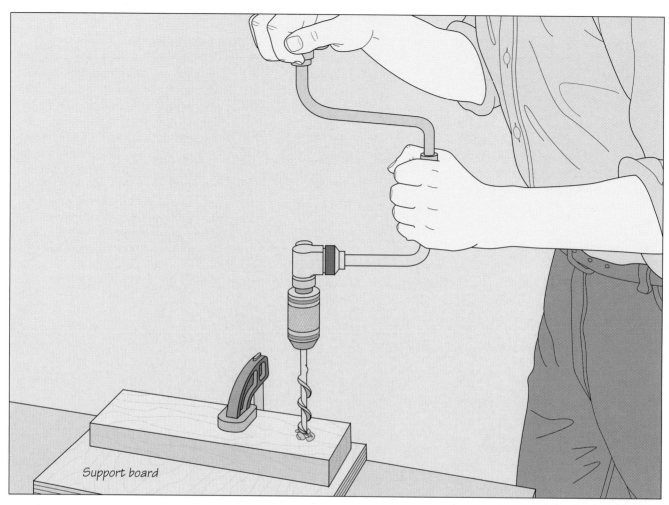

Support board

2 Boring the hole

Clamp the work to the bench on a piece of scrap wood. With the head cupped securely in one hand, grip the handle of the brace firmly and set the tip of the bit on the mark of the hole to be bored, or into the starting hole. Crank the handle clockwise to bore the hole, applying downward pressure on the head of the brace *(above)*. For greater power, set the brace head against your forehead or chest, and bear down on the workpiece. To ensure that the brace is vertical when you bore, you may set a try square beside the bit when you work and keep the two tools parallel.

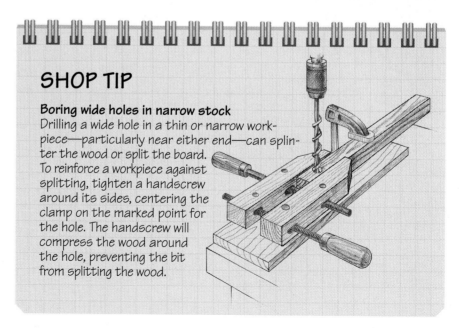

SHOP TIP

Boring wide holes in narrow stock
Drilling a wide hole in a thin or narrow workpiece—particularly near either end—can splinter the wood or split the board. To reinforce a workpiece against splitting, tighten a handscrew around its sides, centering the clamp on the marked point for the hole. The handscrew will compress the wood around the hole, preventing the bit from splitting the wood.

BORING WIDE HOLES

1 Setting up an expansive bit
To adjust the bit to bore a hole of the appropriate diameter, loosen the setscrew on the back of the bit and turn the dial on the front until the correct increment on the cutter's ruler lines up with the gauge line. To check the adjustment, use a ruler; the distance between the spur on the cutter and the center of the bit's lead screw will equal the radius of the hole *(right)*. Tighten the setscrew and recheck the adjustment.

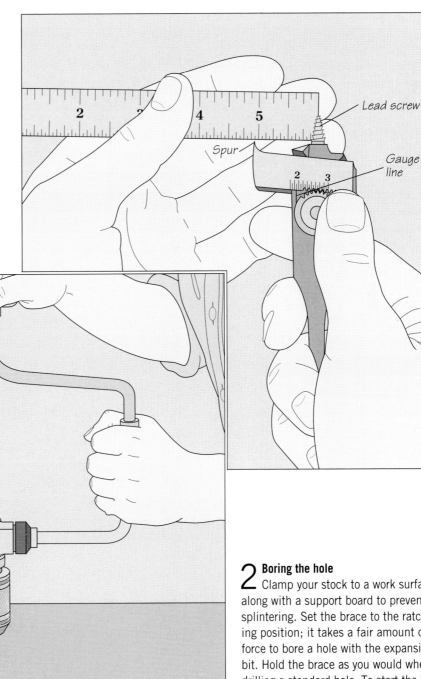

Lead screw

Spur

Gauge line

2 Boring the hole
Clamp your stock to a work surface along with a support board to prevent splintering. Set the brace to the ratcheting position; it takes a fair amount of force to bore a hole with the expansive bit. Hold the brace as you would when drilling a standard hole. To start the hole, crank the handle with a few short strokes until the cutting spur scores the outline of the hole *(left)*. You will need to apply a considerable amount of pressure on the head of the brace to keep the bit from wobbling or moving out of alignment as you complete the hole.

HOLES FOR SCREWS AND PLUGS

Boring holes for screws

Before driving a screw into dense wood, first drill a hole into the workpieces. You may need up to three holes of different diameters, one inside the next. If you want the screw head to sit on the surface of the wood, drill a pilot hole for the threads and a clearance hole for the shank. The pilot hole should be slightly smaller than the screw threads. To set the head flush with the surface, bore a countersink hole *(far right)*. Make it a counterbore hole *(near right)* if you need to conceal the screw with a plug. There is no prescribed sequence for boring these holes, but for a countersink hole, the order shown below and on the facing page is preferred by many woodworkers. If you are drilling a counterbore hole, begin with the counterbore, then drill the clearance and pilot holes.

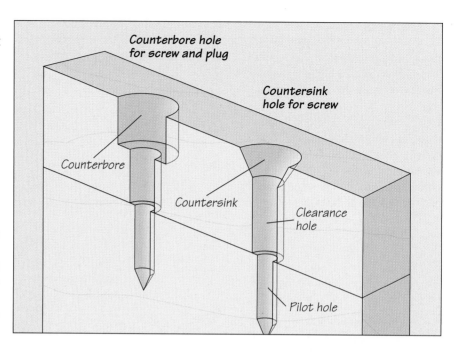

Counterbore hole for screw and plug

Countersink hole for screw

Counterbore

Countersink

Clearance hole

Pilot hole

DRIVING SCREWS

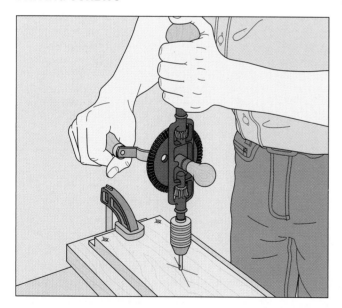

1 Boring a clearance hole
Clamp the workpiece to a work surface, setting a support board under it to prevent splintering. Fit a hand drill with a fluted bit slightly smaller than the screw shank. Press down on the drill's top handle with your thumb and turn the crank handle to bore the hole *(above)*. This depth should equal the length of the screw collar. Be sure to keep the drill perfectly square to the workpiece throughout the operation.

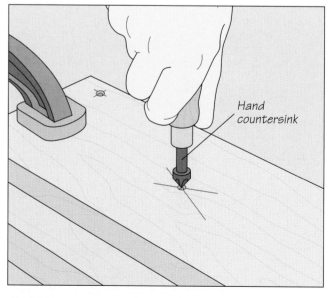

Hand countersink

2 Adding a countersink hole
Once all the clearance holes have been drilled, bore the countersinks. Holding a hand countersink firmly, set the tip in a clearance hole *(above)* and twist it to widen the mouth of the hole. The countersink must be the same diameter as the screw head and its depth should equal the thickness of the head; test for fit with the screw head.

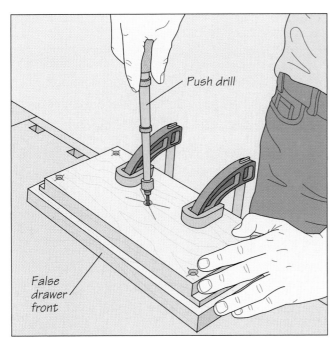

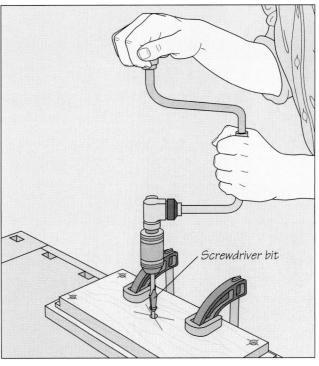

3 Drilling a pilot hole

Remove the clamps, put the support board aside, align the workpieces to be fastened together and clamp them. (In the illustration, a drawer front is being attached to a false front.) Fit a push drill with a fluted bit of a diameter slightly smaller than the screw threads and bore the pilot hole to about the length of the threads *(above)*.

4 Driving the screw

Set the screw in the hole by hand, then install a screwdriver bit in the brace. Fit the bit into the screw head and, holding the brace as you would to bore a hole, crank the handle to drive the screw *(above)*.

SHOP TIP

Protecting wood surfaces
Screwdriver bits being turned by a brace can slip off a screw head. To avoid damaging a workpiece, cut a small piece of perforated hardboard and use a bit to enlarge one of its holes so that it is larger than a screw head. Then, before tightening the screw with the brace, slip the hardboard over the head. If the bit slips off, it will strike the hardboard rather than the workpiece.

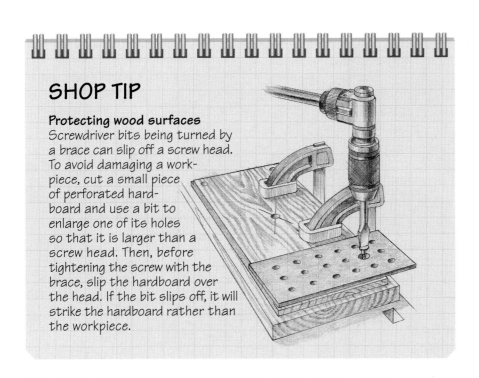

SMOOTHING AND SHAPING TOOLS

A shooting board holds the mitered end of a piece of molding square to the sole of a block plane. Such shop-made jigs extend the versatility of hand planes, letting them smooth end grain with little risk of tearout.

It is hard to imagine building even the simplest piece of furniture without using such tools as hand planes, scrapers, files, and rasps. In fact, most woodworkers—even those with a full complement of power tools—rely on these smoothing tools at different stages of their projects, from the coarse removal of stock to final shaping of decorative details.

The range of these tools is as varied as the tasks they are called upon to perform. Surface-forming tools, such as files and rasps, give initial shape to rough blanks. An inshave is unsurpassed for hollowing out the surface of a panel—a chair seat, for example. A spokeshave can help transform a block of hardwood into an elegant item such as a cabriole leg. A drawknife will debark a log or shape a chair leg. For fine work, there is an equally impressive array of shaping tools, including rifflers, needle rasps, and needle files, to add the finishing touches to a contoured surface, like the foot of a Queen Anne leg. A hand scraper is invaluable for smoothing or for clearing away dried adhesive after glue-up.

Planes are most often used to joint faces and edges prior to glue-up or to prepare surfaces for a finish. For most work, you will need three of the basic bench planes illustrated on page 82: a smoothing plane for surfacing faces and edges, a jointing plane for straightening out longer boards, and a block plane for smoothing end grain. A battery of specially designed planes will make more advanced work possible— from beveling panel edges to cutting dadoes and grooves. The combination plane *(page 98)*, a forerunner of the electric-powered router, comes with a wide range of interchangeable cutters that enable it to shape moldings or cut tongues and matching grooves.

Bench planes are available in two configurations. Steel-bodied planes are the modern standard: solid, accurate, and comfortable to use. Wooden planes are still prized by many woodworkers. Although they are built of an age-old material, today's wooden planes have a modern blade adjustment that makes them every bit as accurate and easy to use as their steel counterparts—while imparting a measure of classical comfort that their users claim is unattainable with any other tool. With a good plane blade and cap iron along with a block of hardwood, you can build your own plane in the shop *(page 94)*, creating a tool that will smooth as finely and accurately as any store-bought model.

The adjustable, flexible sole of a circle plane allows the tool to follow the contoured edges of a tabletop.

ANATOMIES OF TWO BENCH PLANES

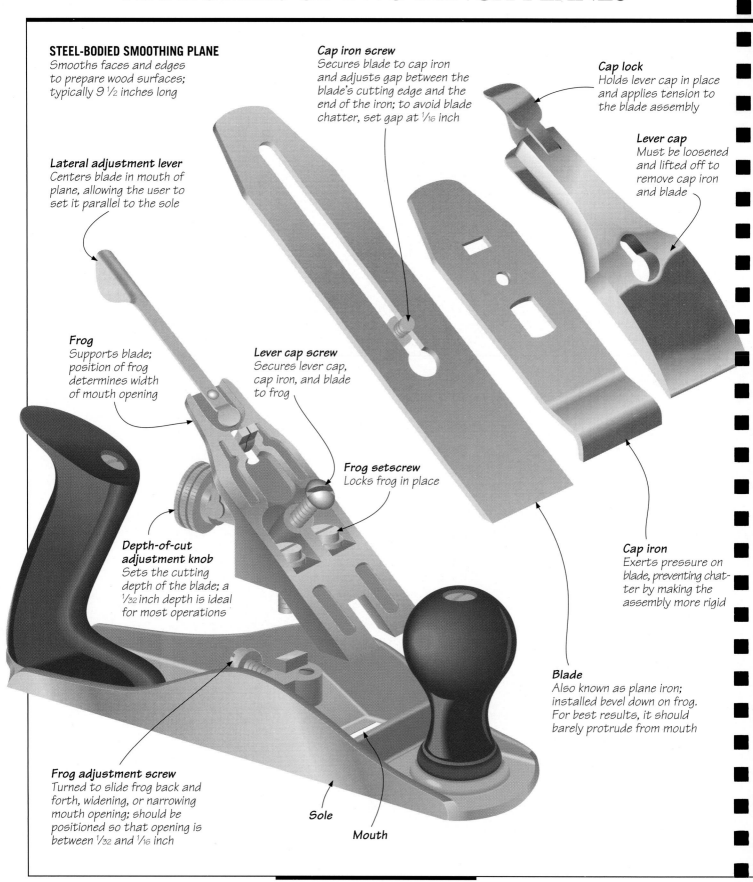

STEEL-BODIED SMOOTHING PLANE
Smooths faces and edges to prepare wood surfaces; typically 9 ½ inches long

Cap iron screw
Secures blade to cap iron and adjusts gap between the blade's cutting edge and the end of the iron; to avoid blade chatter, set gap at 1/16 inch

Cap lock
Holds lever cap in place and applies tension to the blade assembly

Lever cap
Must be loosened and lifted off to remove cap iron and blade

Lateral adjustment lever
Centers blade in mouth of plane, allowing the user to set it parallel to the sole

Frog
Supports blade; position of frog determines width of mouth opening

Lever cap screw
Secures lever cap, cap iron, and blade to frog

Frog setscrew
Locks frog in place

Depth-of-cut adjustment knob
Sets the cutting depth of the blade; a 1/32 inch depth is ideal for most operations

Cap iron
Exerts pressure on blade, preventing chatter by making the assembly more rigid

Blade
Also known as plane iron; installed bevel down on frog. For best results, it should barely protrude from mouth

Frog adjustment screw
Turned to slide frog back and forth, widening, or narrowing mouth opening; should be positioned so that opening is between 1/32 and 1/16 inch

Sole

Mouth

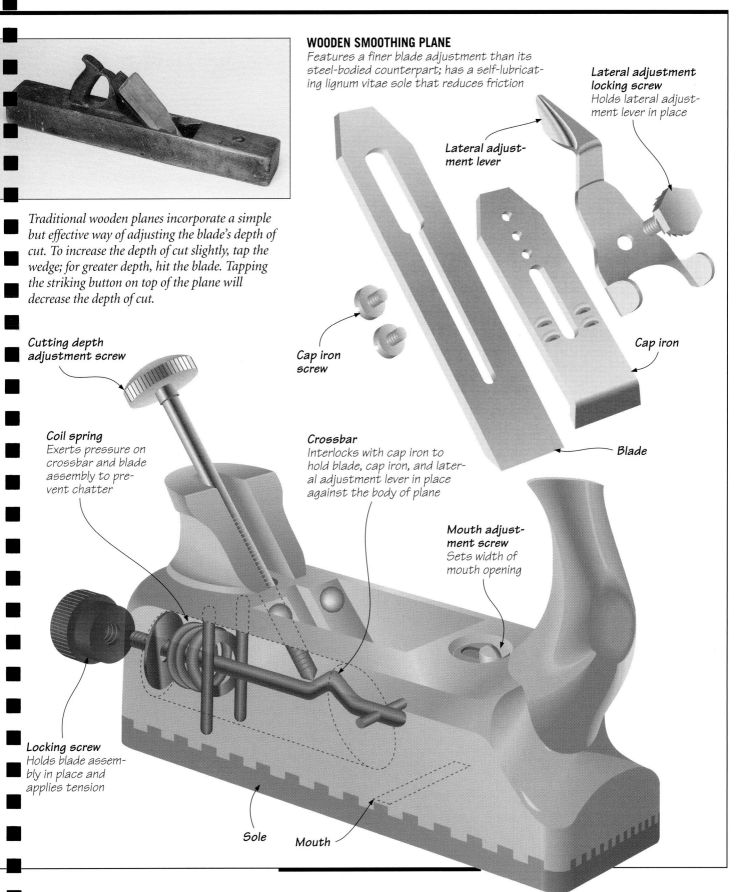

WOODEN SMOOTHING PLANE
Features a finer blade adjustment than its steel-bodied counterpart; has a self-lubricating lignum vitae sole that reduces friction

Traditional wooden planes incorporate a simple but effective way of adjusting the blade's depth of cut. To increase the depth of cut slightly, tap the wedge; for greater depth, hit the blade. Tapping the striking button on top of the plane will decrease the depth of cut.

Lateral adjustment locking screw
Holds lateral adjustment lever in place

Lateral adjustment lever

Cap iron

Cap iron screw

Blade

Cutting depth adjustment screw

Coil spring
Exerts pressure on crossbar and blade assembly to prevent chatter

Crossbar
Interlocks with cap iron to hold blade, cap iron, and lateral adjustment lever in place against the body of plane

Mouth adjustment screw
Sets width of mouth opening

Locking screw
Holds blade assembly in place and applies tension

Sole

Mouth

PLANES

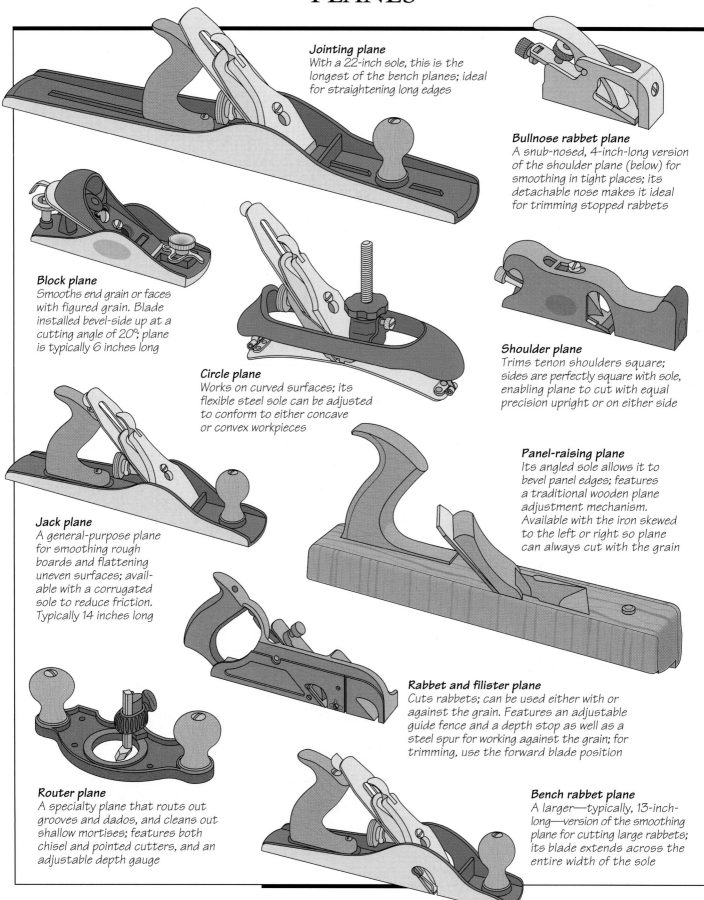

Jointing plane
With a 22-inch sole, this is the longest of the bench planes; ideal for straightening long edges

Bullnose rabbet plane
A snub-nosed, 4-inch-long version of the shoulder plane (below) for smoothing in tight places; its detachable nose makes it ideal for trimming stopped rabbets

Block plane
Smooths end grain or faces with figured grain. Blade installed bevel-side up at a cutting angle of 20°; plane is typically 6 inches long

Circle plane
Works on curved surfaces; its flexible steel sole can be adjusted to conform to either concave or convex workpieces

Shoulder plane
Trims tenon shoulders square; sides are perfectly square with sole, enabling plane to cut with equal precision upright or on either side

Jack plane
A general-purpose plane for smoothing rough boards and flattening uneven surfaces; available with a corrugated sole to reduce friction. Typically 14 inches long

Panel-raising plane
Its angled sole allows it to bevel panel edges; features a traditional wooden plane adjustment mechanism. Available with the iron skewed to the left or right so plane can always cut with the grain

Rabbet and filister plane
Cuts rabbets; can be used either with or against the grain. Features an adjustable guide fence and a depth stop as well as a steel spur for working against the grain; for trimming, use the forward blade position

Router plane
A specialty plane that routs out grooves and dados, and cleans out shallow mortises; features both chisel and pointed cutters, and an adjustable depth gauge

Bench rabbet plane
A larger—typically, 13-inch-long—version of the smoothing plane for cutting large rabbets; its blade extends across the entire width of the sole

A plane must be sharp and properly adjusted to shear off shavings of wood—often as thin as paper—with no tearout. Before using a new plane you will have to sharpen the blade and adjust the tool for top performance. The procedure involves two steps: creating a bevel on the blade's cutting edge and honing another bevel on part of the first one, called a microbevel; then removing, or "lapping," the burr that results from the honing process.

If the cutting edge is damaged in any way, or if you are trying to restore an old blade, you first need to square its end. As shown in the photo at right, a grinder is the best tool to use for this purpose.

Whether you work with steel-bodied or wooden planes, setting them up requires very little in the way of special-

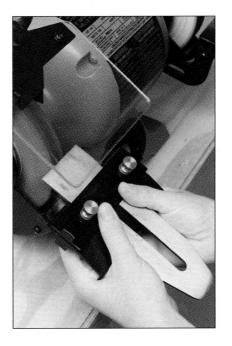

ized equipment. Honing can be accomplished with a combination sharpening stone and a commercial honing guide. Adjusting a plane's depth of cut requires only a screwdriver. The sole of a wooden plane becomes naturally slick with use; however, rubbing a little paste wax on the bottom of a steel-bodied plane will reduce friction.

Hone your blades frequently to maintain a keen edge and always retract them into the plane after use. Store the plane upright to prevent the sole from being harmed by other tools.

A nicked or out-of-square plane blade can be salvaged by squaring its end on a grinder. The guide helps keep the blade perpendicular to the grinding wheel.

HONING A PLANE BLADE

Bevel

Microbevel

OIL

Honing
guide

Sharpening stone

1 Creating a bevel and honing a microbevel

Place a combination sharpening stone coarse side up on a work surface. Nail cleats to the table against the stone to keep it from moving. Clamp the blade top face up in a commercial honing guide set for a 30° bevel. Saturate the stone with the appropriate lubricant—either water or a light oil—until it pools on the surface. Then, holding the honing guide, slide the blade back and forth from end to end along the stone *(left)*, grinding the bevel. To hone the microbevel, reposition the blade in the guide, raise the angle by 5°, and turn the stone over. Saturate the stone again and repeat the process, applying moderate pressure until a microbevel forms *(inset)*.

2 Lapping the burr

To remove the burr—a thin ridge of metal that forms on the flat face of the blade as a result of honing the microbevel—remove the blade from the honing guide and saturate the fine side of the stone once again. Holding the blade perfectly flat on the stone, bevel side up *(above)*, move it in a circular pattern on the stone until the flat side of the cutting edge is smooth. Test the sharpness of the cutting edge on a piece of paper; a sharp blade will slice a sliver from the paper's edge.

SHOP TIP

A shop-made honing jig
If you do not own a commercial honing guide, you can still get good results sharpening plane blades using this simple jig. Slip a 4-inch-long, 3/8-inch-diameter carriage bolt through the blade's slot. Fasten with washers and wing nuts on both sides of the blade. With the blade on the sharpening stone and the head of the bolt on your work surface, use a protractor and a sliding bevel to adjust the wing nuts so that the blade can be slid along the stone at the proper angle.

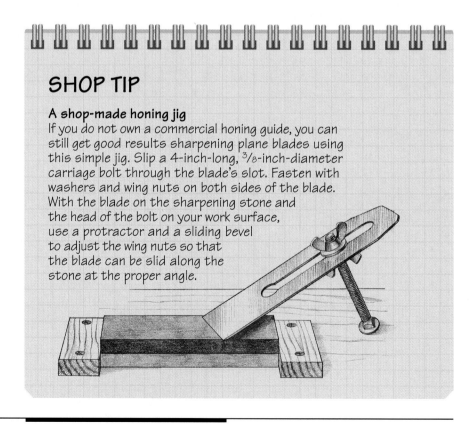

ADJUSTING A PLANE

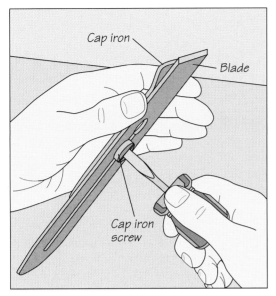

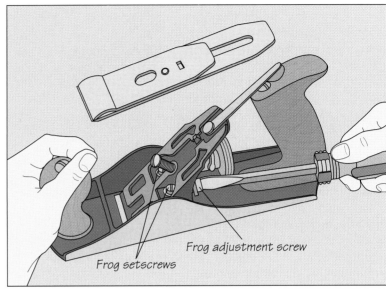

1 Positioning the blade assembly

Position the cap iron on the top face of the blade with the cutting edge of the blade extending about 1/16 inch beyond the end of the cap iron. Tighten the cap iron screw *(above, left)*. Then place the blade assembly—including the blade, cap iron and lever cap—in position on the frog. The gap between the front edge of the blade and the front of the mouth should be between 1/32 and 1/16 inch. If the gap is too wide or narrow, remove the blade assembly and loosen both frog setscrews about 1/4 turn. Then adjust the frog adjustment screw to set the proper gap *(above, right)*. Tighten the setscrews and reposition the blade assembly on the frog, locking it in place with the cap lock.

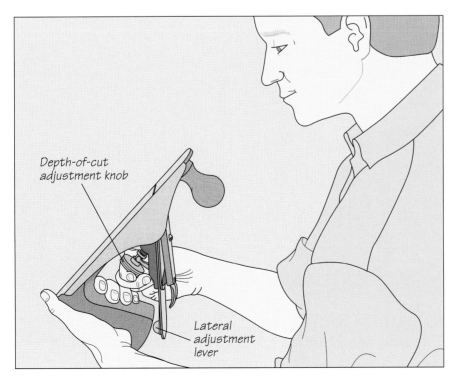

2 Centering the blade and adjusting the depth of cut

Holding the plane upside down, move the lateral adjustment lever so that the cutting edge is level and centered in the mouth. To set the cutting depth, turn the depth-of-cut adjustment knob so that the blade protrudes from the mouth, usually about 1/32 inch is desirable *(left)*—less for highly figured woods. Confirm the setting with a test cut on a scrap board. The shavings should be paper-thin.

BASIC TECHNIQUES

H and planing procedures are the same regardless of what type or size of bench plane you use. Guide the tool along the surface by pushing it away from you with smooth, even strokes. (If you are using a Japanese plane, remember that it cuts on the pull, rather than the push, stroke.) Align your shoulder and hip with the plane, and grip the tool with both hands. Cup one hand around the front knob and keep the other at the back—either around the handle or the body.

Apply firm, constant pressure with every stroke. To keep the sole of the plane flat, exert more downward pressure on the front of the tool at the beginning of the stroke and shift the pressure to the rear as you approach the end. Your stock should always be clamped to a work surface.

Its blade adjusted to slice off the thinnest of shavings, a wooden smoothing plane evens out the surface of a workpiece.

It is important that you cut with the grain of the wood. You can usually determine the grain direction by running your hand along the board face or edge: The surface will feel smoother when your hand is moving with the grain and rougher when running against it. Another method is to make a test cut: The blade will chatter or catch on the wood when it is cutting against the grain.

PLANING WITH THE WOOD GRAIN

Choosing the direction to plane

Determine the grain slope by inspecting the surface adjoining the one you are planing. The diagram at right shows several typical grain patterns with arrows indicating the best direction to plane. The direction may be constant from one end of a board to the other (A). Or it may change, requiring that you plane the surface from each end toward the middle (B) or from middle toward each end (C). If the grain does not slope at all, you can plane the surface in a single pass from either end (D). With irregular grain, guiding the plane at a slight angle to the direction of travel will help reduce the tearout by shearing the wood rather than tearing it. If you must plane against the grain, set the depth of cut to remove the thinnest possible shaving.

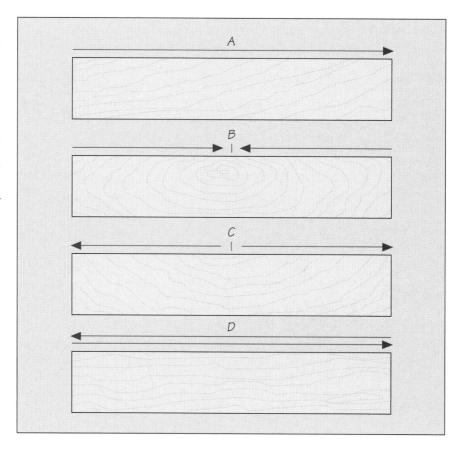

PLANING A FACE

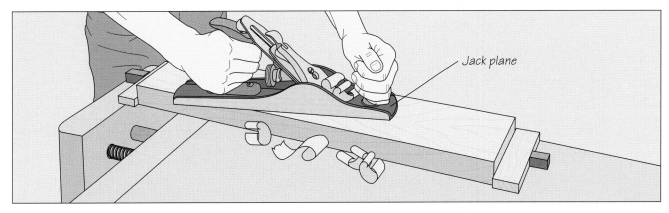

Jack plane

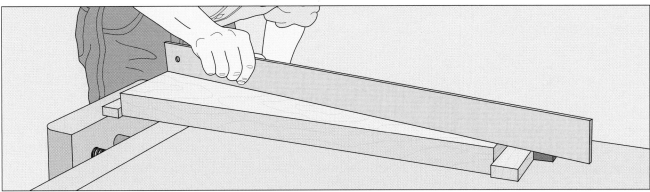

SHOP TIP

Checking for flatness with a bench plane
If the sides of your plane are perfectly square to the sole, you can use it instead of a straightedge to determine whether a surface is flat. Simply tip the tool on edge and hold it on the surface at several points. If the plane rests flush along its entire length, the surface is flat.

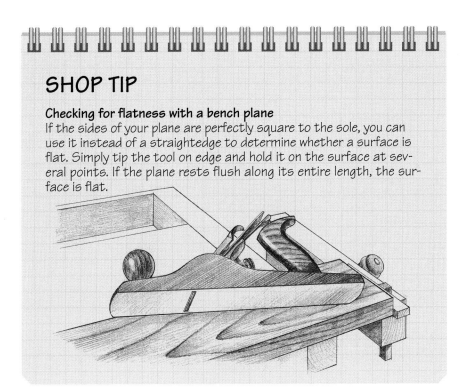

Using a jack plane
Secure your stock face up on a work surface. Once you have oriented the plane with the wood grain, set the sole on the board with the blade just clear of one end. To remove stock quickly, plane with smooth, even strokes, angling the tool slightly to the grain *(above, top)*. To smooth the surface, keep the plane parallel to the grain, using a series of straight passes that slightly overlap. Examine the shavings as you work and adjust the cutting depth if you want a finer cut. Keep planing until the surface is smooth and shiny. To check whether the surface is flat, hold a straightedge across the face at several points *(above, bottom)*. The straightedge should rest flush against the surface. If there is a gap, plane the high spots and recheck.

SMOOTHING EDGES

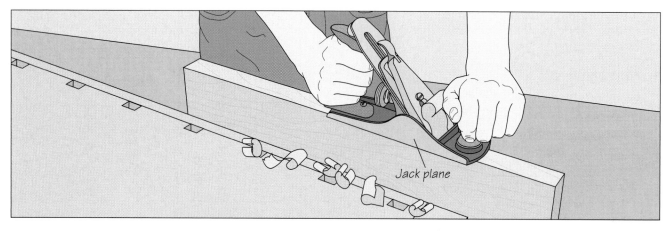

Jack plane

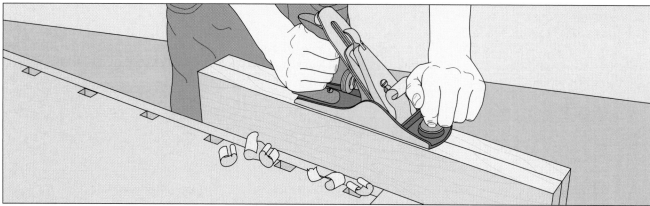

Planing edges square

Secure the workpiece edge up in a vise. Guide a jack plane along the edge from one end of the board to the other, keeping the sole straight and flat on the surface *(above, top)*. To help steady the plane, you can press down on the toe with the thumb of your forward hand and curl your fingers around the face of the workpiece as you make the pass. If you need to plane the edges of several workpieces, secure them face to face in the vise, aligning their ends and edges. Then smooth their surfaces together *(above, bottom)* as you would a single board.

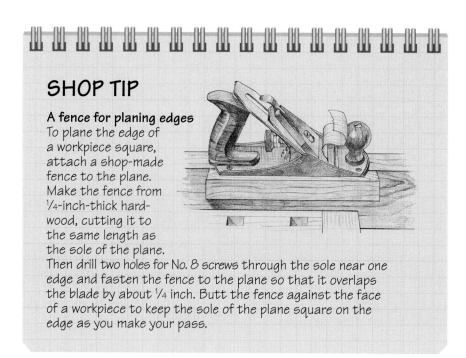

SHOP TIP

A fence for planing edges
To plane the edge of a workpiece square, attach a shop-made fence to the plane. Make the fence from 1/4-inch-thick hardwood, cutting it to the same length as the sole of the plane. Then drill two holes for No. 8 screws through the sole near one edge and fasten the fence to the plane so that it overlaps the blade by about 1/4 inch. Butt the fence against the face of a workpiece to keep the sole of the plane square on the edge as you make your pass.

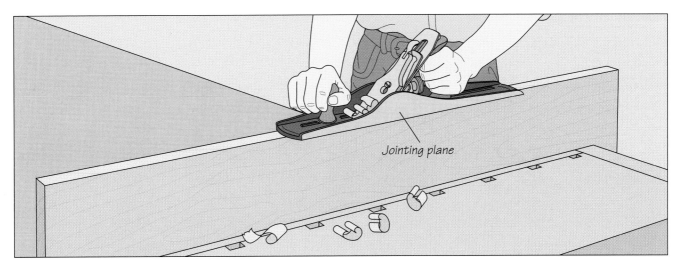

Straightening out a long edge

To plane the edge of a long workpiece, use a jointing plane. Its long sole makes it less likely than a jack plane to follow the contours that you want to remove. Secure the workpiece with the edge facing up; clamp one end to the workbench if neces-sary to keep the board steady. Starting at one end, guide the plane along the edge *(above)*, walking next to the workpiece until you reach the other end. Make as many passes as neces-sary until the plane slices off one long shaving from end to end.

BUILD IT YOURSELF

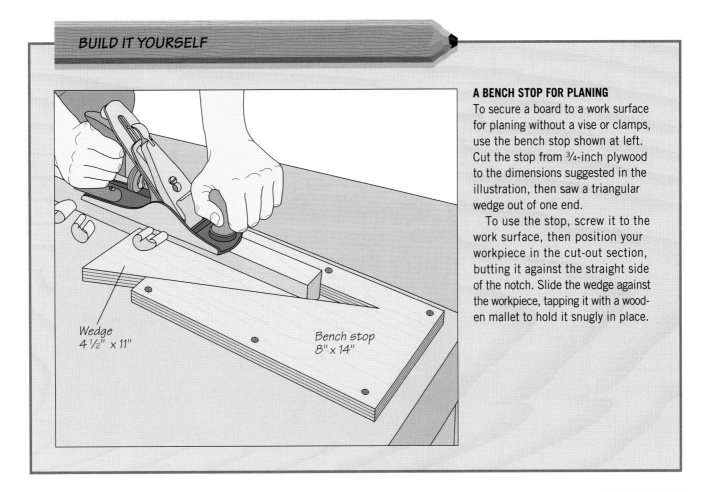

Wedge
4 1/2" x 11"

Bench stop
8" x 14"

A BENCH STOP FOR PLANING

To secure a board to a work surface for planing without a vise or clamps, use the bench stop shown at left. Cut the stop from 3/4-inch plywood to the dimensions suggested in the illustration, then saw a triangular wedge out of one end.

To use the stop, screw it to the work surface, then position your workpiece in the cut-out section, butting it against the straight side of the notch. Slide the wedge against the workpiece, tapping it with a wood-en mallet to hold it snugly in place.

PLANING END GRAIN

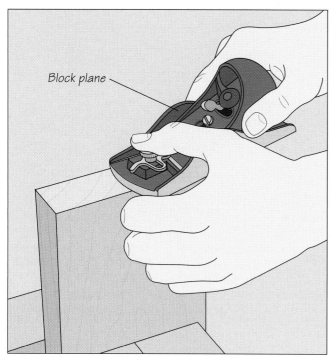

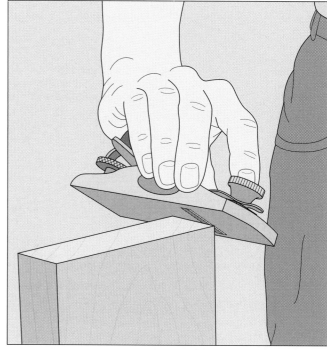

Smoothing end grain

Use a block plane to smooth the ends of a workpiece. There are three ways to do the job without causing tearout at the end of each cut. Two are shown above; a third method is shown below. Start by securing the workpiece end-up in a vise. For the first method, work toward the center, beginning at one edge of the board with the plane held at an angle to the sides. Guide the tool along the surface until the blade is about halfway across the end *(above, left)*, then repeat the process from the opposite edge. For the second method, cut a chamfer: Hold the plane at an angle to flatten the corner *(above, right)*. Then make a pass along the entire end, beginning the stroke at the other edge.

Using a support block

A third method of smoothing end grain allows you to make each pass with a single stroke. Secure the workpiece end up with support blocks clamped to both edges as shown. The blocks should be the same thickness as the workpiece; the one at the end of the pass should be level with the end to be planed. Guide the plane along the surface from one edge to the other, holding the tool at a slight angle to the sides of the board *(right)*.

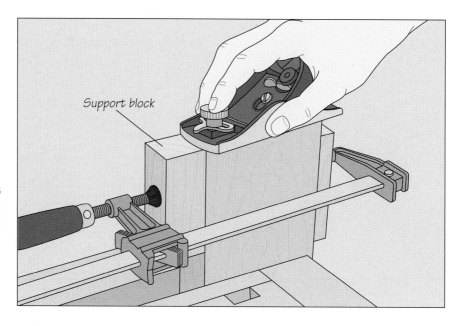

BUILD IT YOURSELF

SHOOTING BOARDS

To smooth end grain using a jack plane, use a shooting board like those shown at right. The right-angle shooting board is for planing straight end grain; the angled version can be used to smooth mitered ends. Cut the pieces according to the dimensions suggested in the illustration. Build the base, top, and mitered stop block from ¾-inch plywood; use hardwood for the lip and square stop block.

Screw the top to the base with the ends and one edge aligned. Then attach the lip to the base, making sure that the lip lines up with the edge of the base. Fasten the right-angled stop block to the top flush with the other edge of the jig. Center the mitered stop block on the top.

To use either jig, hook the lip over the edge of a work surface. Set your workpiece on the top, butting the edge against the stop block so that it extends over the edge of the top by about $\frac{1}{16}$ inch. With the mitered shooting board, the workpiece can be positioned against either side of the stop block. Place a support under the opposite end of the board to be planed to keep it level. Holding the workpiece steady, set a jack plane on its side at one end of the jig, butting the sole against the edge of the top. Guide the plane along the jig (*right, below*) from one end to the other.

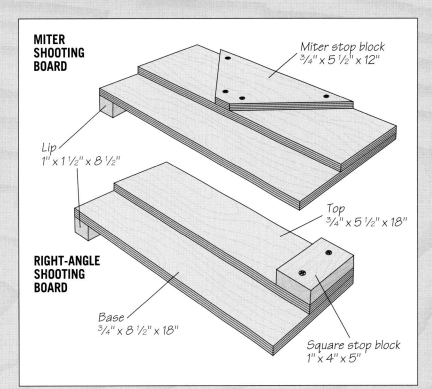

MITER SHOOTING BOARD

Miter stop block
¾" x 5 ½" x 12"

Lip
1" x 1 ½" x 8 ½"

Top
¾" x 5 ½" x 18"

RIGHT-ANGLE SHOOTING BOARD

Base
¾" x 8 ½" x 18"

Square stop block
1" x 4" x 5"

Jack plane

Support board

SALVAGING A BOWED BOARD

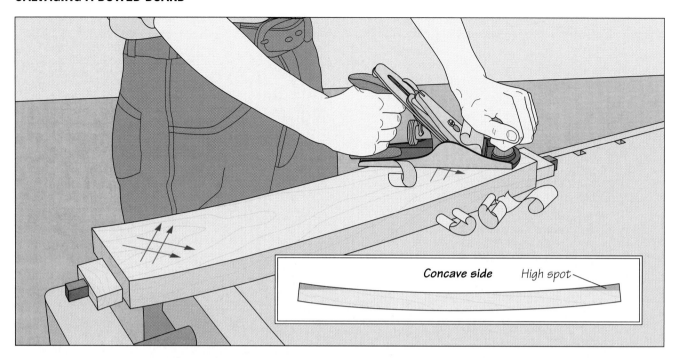

Concave side   High spot

Convex side

Planing a bowed board flat

Salvage a bowed board in two steps using a jack plane. First, secure the workpiece with its concave face up and shave away the high spots near the ends of the board *(inset, top)*. Guide the plane at a 45° angle to the grain, alternating the direction of your strokes by 90°, as shown by the red arrows *(above, top)*. Once the surface is flat, turn the workpiece over and repeat the process *(above, bottom)*. This time, you will be removing a single high spot in the middle of the board *(inset, bottom)*.

TROUBLESHOOTING PLANING PROBLEMS

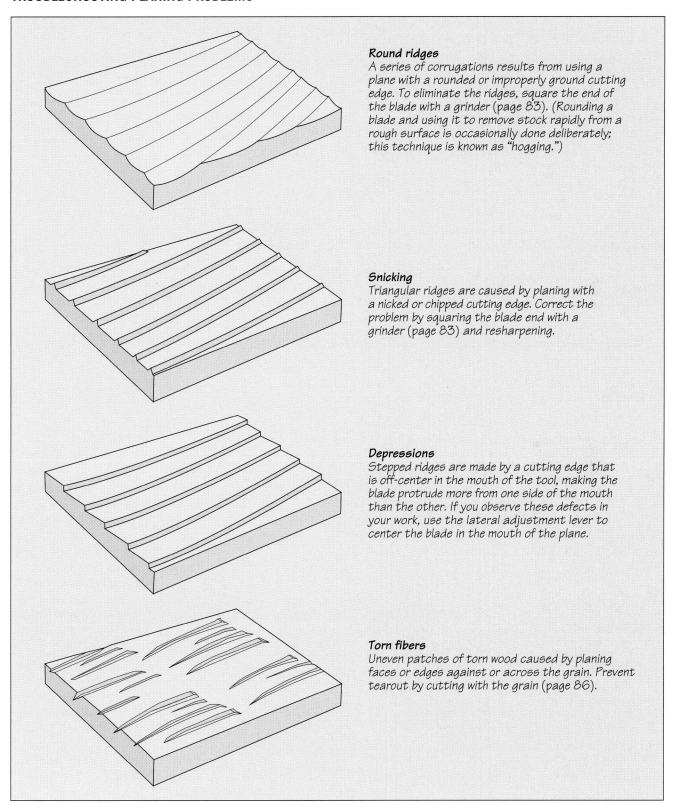

Round ridges
A series of corrugations results from using a plane with a rounded or improperly ground cutting edge. To eliminate the ridges, square the end of the blade with a grinder (page 83). (Rounding a blade and using it to remove stock rapidly from a rough surface is occasionally done deliberately; this technique is known as "hogging.")

Snicking
Triangular ridges are caused by planing with a nicked or chipped cutting edge. Correct the problem by squaring the blade end with a grinder (page 83) and resharpening.

Depressions
Stepped ridges are made by a cutting edge that is off-center in the mouth of the tool, making the blade protrude more from one side of the mouth than the other. If you observe these defects in your work, use the lateral adjustment lever to center the blade in the mouth of the plane.

Torn fibers
Uneven patches of torn wood caused by planing faces or edges against or across the grain. Prevent tearout by cutting with the grain (page 86).

BUILD IT YOURSELF

A BENCH PLANE

Although commercial steel bench planes look difficult to duplicate, you can build a wooden version in the shop that will cut as accurately as any store-bought tool. The parts list is straightforward: a hardwood block, a good plane blade and cap iron, and lengths of dowel.

The jointing plane shown at right was made using the "sandwich" method. First, a sole was glued on the bottom, then two cheeks were cut off the sides of the hardwood blank destined to become the plane body. The mortise for the blade and cap iron was sawn out next. Finally, the cheeks were glued back on to the body, and the blade and cap iron were put in place, held fast by a wooden wedge.

Start by cutting the blank for the body to size. Choose a dense, close-grained hardwood like maple or box-

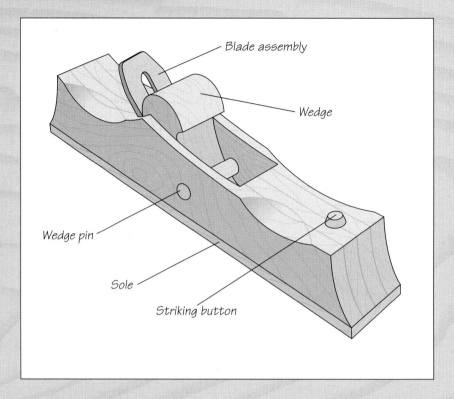

wood. If you cannot find a solid block of wood, glue up individual boards to the required dimensions (as was done for the illustrated plane). The size of the blank depends on the type of plane you wish to build. Smoothing planes are typically 7 to 9 inches long; jack planes range between 14 and 18 inches in length. The plane in the illustration is 18 inches long, but a jointing plane can be as long as 24 inches. Add 4 inches to the finished length you want. Make the blank 1½ inches wider than the blade. If you are building a smoothing plane, cut the blank 3 to 4 inches high; for a jack or jointing plane, make it 4 or 5 inches high.

Once the blank is cut to size, joint the bottom and glue on a sole. Use an oily and dense hardwood like cocobolo

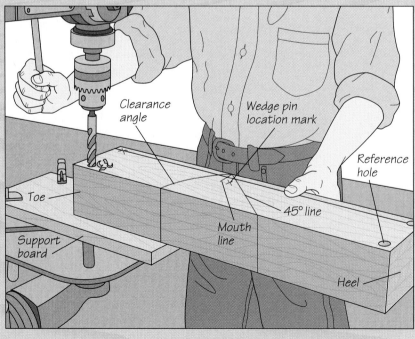

or lignum vitae for the sole, cutting it slightly longer and wider than the blank and at least ¼ inch thick. Attach the sole so that the uphill direction of the grain runs from the heel to the toe. Once the glue is dry, trim the excess wood from the sole and square the blank.

Next, mark out the blade mortise as shown on page 94 *(bottom)*. Mark a line across the sole for the mouth of the plane, placing it about one-third of the way from the toe. Then, from one end of this line, draw a line across one side of the blank at a 45° angle to the sole toward the heel. Then start another line from the same point, curving it gently toward the toe to form a clearance angle for the mortise. Transfer these lines across the top of the blank to the other side. Next, extend the mouth line up the sides 1¾ inches. Then measure horizontally ¾ inch back toward the heel and mark the center of the wedge pin. Finally, mark a location point for a reference dowel inside each corner of the blank. The marks should be close enough to the ends so that they can be cut off when the

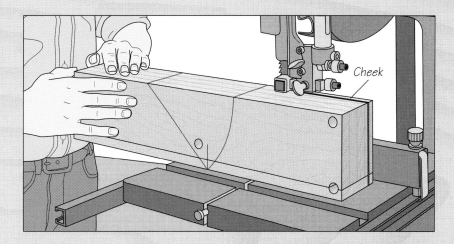

Cheek

plane is trimmed to its finished size.

Place the blank on its side on a drill press table, clamping a support board underneath to prevent splintering when the bit exits the blank. Bore ½-inch-diameter holes at the corner marks *(page 94, bottom)* and a ¾-inch-diameter hole at the wedge pin location mark. Next, install a ¾-inch-wide resaw blade on the band saw and set up the rip fence on the table for a ½-inch-wide cut. Feed the blank into the blade with both hands to cut off one cheek, keeping the side flush against the

fence and the sole flat on the table *(above)*. Repeat to cut a cheek from the other side of the blank, then set the cheeks aside.

Plane the sides of the blank until it is no more than 1/16 inch wider than the plane blade. Redraw the lines for the blade mortise on the sides of the blank, then install a 3/8-inch-wide blade on the band saw. Align the blade with one of the lines at the top of the blank, then feed the blank on its side into the blade using your right hand, while guiding it with your left hand *(left)*. Cut as close as possible to the point where the two marked lines meet but do not saw completely through the sole. Repeat to cut along the other line. Remove the waste piece and set it aside; later, you will fashion the piece into the blade wedge. Separate the blank into two pieces by hand and lightly sand the surfaces of the blade mortise.

To prepare the pieces for reassembly, test fit the cap iron and blade on the heel piece of the blank and mark the location of the cap iron screw. Then cut a groove for the screw *(page 96, top)*, stopping it 2 inches above the

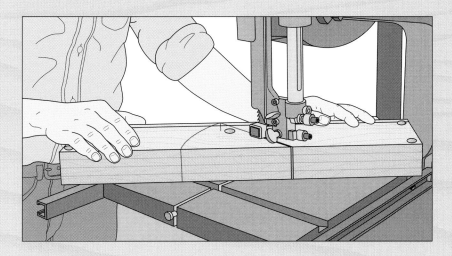

BUILD IT YOURSELF (continued)

mouth of the plane. Glue the cheeks back onto the blank, inserting lengths of ½-inch-diameter dowel into the reference holes in the sides of the cheeks to help align the pieces accurately *(right)*. Clamp the assembly together securely. Once the glue is dry, remove the clamps and cut off the doweled ends of the blank.

Next, prepare the wedge and wedge pin. Cut the wedge from the waste piece you sawed out of the blank. The bottom of the wedge should taper to a point, the surface that rests against the blade and cap iron should be flat, and the top should be rounded. For the wedge pin, cut a ¾-inch dowel to the same length as the width of the plane body. File a flat surface on one side of the pin large enough to accommodate the wedge.

Use the jointer to fine-tune the mouth opening of your plane. Set up the machine for a ¹⁄₃₂-inch depth of cut and make one pass. Then install the blade, cap iron, wedge, and wedge pin in the body and measure the distance from the cutting edge to

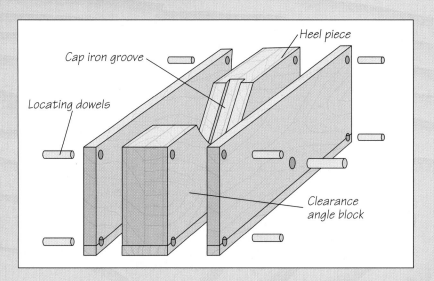

Cap iron groove

Heel piece

Locating dowels

Clearance angle block

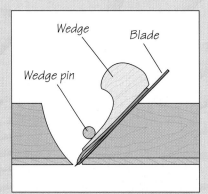

Wedge

Blade

Wedge pin

the bottom of the sole. Your goal is a ¹⁄₁₆-inch space, and several passes through the jointer—plane blade and wedge removed—may be necessary. Once the space is right, use a chisel to widen the mouth, shaving the front edge of the opening so that the blade just slips through it *(left)*. Check the mouth opening by installing the blade and wedge, and making a pass with the plane on a scrap board. If the shavings jam against the blade, rather than curling up over it, widen the mouth with the chisel.

Once the mouth is perfectly adjusted, you can modify the shape of the plane body to suit your hands. Finally, glue a striking button onto the top of the body near the toe. To loosen the wedge and remove the blade and cap iron from the tool, tap the striking button with a wooden mallet *(left)*. To use the plane, set the blade and cap iron in position at the appropriate cutting depth, and install the wedge and its pin. Tap the wedge with a mallet, making sure it is holding the blade snugly in place.

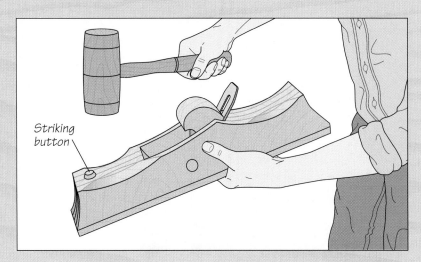

Striking button

Although bench planes can handle a wide variety of smoothing tasks, there is an array of specialty planes available to the woodworker who is faced with more delicate operations, smoothing and trimming wood in out-of-the-way places. From the diminutive bullnose rabbet plane to the large combination plane with its host of interchangeable cutters, each specialty plane is designed to reach a tricky place or plane a difficult surface.

Many of these tools were developed especially for joinery. The rabbet, shoulder, router and bullnose rabbet planes all feature precise blade adjustments that allow you to fine-tune tenons, hinge mortises, dadoes, and grooves—surfaces that are invariably too restricted for even

the most compact bench plane. With the versatile combination plane, you can shape a piece of molding or cut a tongue-and-groove joint, depending on the cutter you install in the tool. A circle plane will smooth the edges of a curved piece as its rounded sole follows the contours of the wood, keeping the blade from taking off too much wood from any point around the circumference.

Although all these planes can be adjusted to a wide range of cutting depths, you rarely should shave more than $1/32$ to $1/16$ inch with each pass of these tools. To ensure precise results, always clamp your stock to a work surface firmly before planing it, remembering to protect the surfaces of the workpiece with wood pads where necessary.

A specialty plane in action: A router plane trims the bottom of a hinge mortise in a cabinet door.

FINE-TUNING A TENON

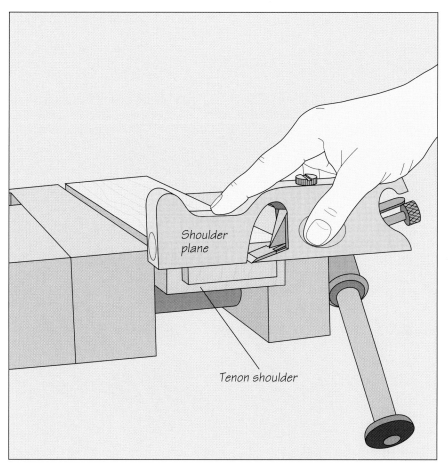

Shoulder plane

Tenon shoulder

Trimming the cheeks and shoulders
Use a shoulder plane to trim a short tenon. Secure the workpiece in a vise with the tenon extending beyond the work surface. Adjust the cutting depth to no more than $1/32$ inch, then hold the side of the plane flush against the shoulder and guide the sole along the cheek *(left)*. Check the fit frequently, making as many light passes as necessary to trim the surface to the correct depth. To trim the tenon shoulder, place the plane on its side and cut along the shoulder while holding the side of the tool flat on the cheek. Turn the workpiece over and repeat the process on the opposite cheek and shoulder. To trim the adjoining sides of the tenon, secure the workpiece edge-up in the vise. For longer tenons, in which the width of the tenon cheek exceeds the width of the shoulder plane's sole, use a bench rabbet plane.

CUTTING A TONGUE-AND-GROOVE JOINT

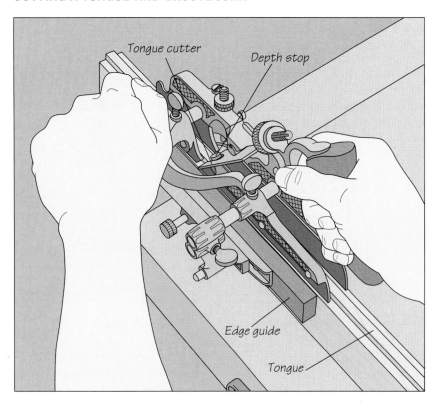

Tongue cutter

Depth stop

Edge guide

Tongue

Cutting the tongue and the groove

Use a multiplane, or combination plane, to cut a tongue and matching groove. Begin with the tongue: Secure one workpiece edge-up and install a tongue cutter in the plane. Adjust the edge guide to center the cutter on the workpiece and set the depth stop to the desired depth of the tongue. Start near the far end of the workpiece and make a shallow cut, keeping the edge guide flush against the stock. Begin the second pass a little closer to you, and continue working your way to the near end until you have cut a shallow tongue along the full length of the edge. Now make full-length passes along the surface *(left)* until you reach the correct depth. To cut the groove, secure the mating work-piece and install a groove cutter of the same width as the tongue cutter in the plane. Set the depth stop to cut the groove slightly deep-er than the tongue, then cut the groove with a series of short, shallow passes the same way you cut the tongue.

The combination plane is a versatile, hand-powered precursor of the router. Its range of interchangeable cutters can form tongues, grooves, dadoes, flutes, reeds, ovolos, and beadings. An adjustable edge guide ensures straight cuts while a depth stop allows the tool to trim to precise depths. The model shown at right, the Stanley 45 Multiplane, is an original design that has inspired many imitators.

CUTTING A RABBET

Using a rabbet and fillister plane

Secure your workpiece to a work surface, protecting the stock with wood pads. Adjust the plane's edge guide for the desired width of the rabbet and set the depth stop located behind the fence for the depth. Cut the rabbet as you would a tongue or groove with the combination plane: Start with short strokes near the far end of the workpiece and gradually work your way to the near end until you have plowed a shallow rabbet. Then make a series of passes along the entire length of the surface *(right)* until the depth stop prevents the blade from cutting further. If you need to plane both across and with the grain, work across the grain first, clamping a support block to the work-piece when planing across the grain to prevent tearout *(page 90)*.

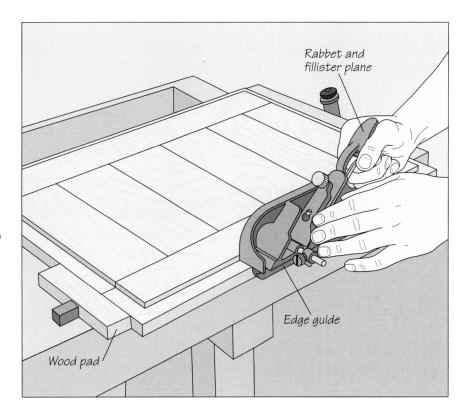

Rabbet and fillister plane

Edge guide

Wood pad

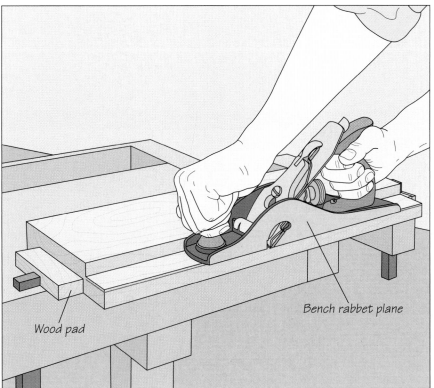

Wood pad

Bench rabbet plane

Using a bench rabbet plane

Since the bench rabbet plane has no built-in edge guide or depth stop, you will need to mark one line on the face of the workpiece for the width of the rabbet and another on the edge for the rabbet's depth. Secure the workpiece and clamp an edge guide to the face of the stock so that it aligns with the rabbet width line. Starting at the near end of the workpiece, make a full-length pass, keeping the side of the plane flush against the edge guide. Continue in this manner until the rabbet is deep enough for its shoulder to guide the plane. Remove the edge guide and continue planing *(left)* until you have cut to the depth line.

TRIMMING A STOPPED RABBET

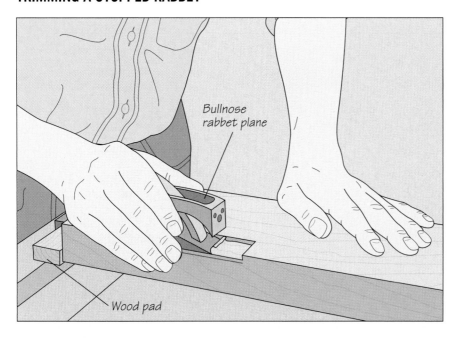

Bullnose
rabbet plane

Wood pad

Leveling the rabbet

A bullnose rabbet plane is designed to trim a stopped rabbet or other enclosed spaces. Secure the workpiece, then unscrew the nose from the front of the plane and set the depth of cut at no more than $1/32$ inch. Starting at the end of the workpiece, guide the plane along the surface to the other end of the rabbet *(left)*, keeping the side of plane flush against the rabbet shoulder. Make as many passes as necessary to trim the rabbet to the appropriate depth.

CUTTING A DADO

Making the cut

Cut a dado using a router plane. Clamp the workpiece face-up, then mark two sets of cutting lines: one on the face for the width of the dado and another on the edge for the dado depth. Saw a kerf along each of the dado width lines, stopping the cuts at the depth line. Then install a chisel cutter on the plane. Loosen the depth adjustment knob and set the cutting depth to about $1/16$ inch; tighten the knob. Begin each pass with the plane at the far edge of the workpiece and pull the tool toward you *(right)*. Keep the cutter flat on the surface and aligned between the saw kerfs. Increase the cutting depth of the plane after each pass, continuing until you reach the depth mark.

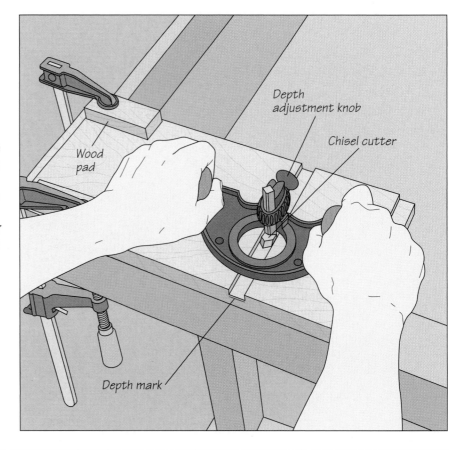

Wood pad

Depth adjustment knob

Chisel cutter

Depth mark

RAISING A PANEL

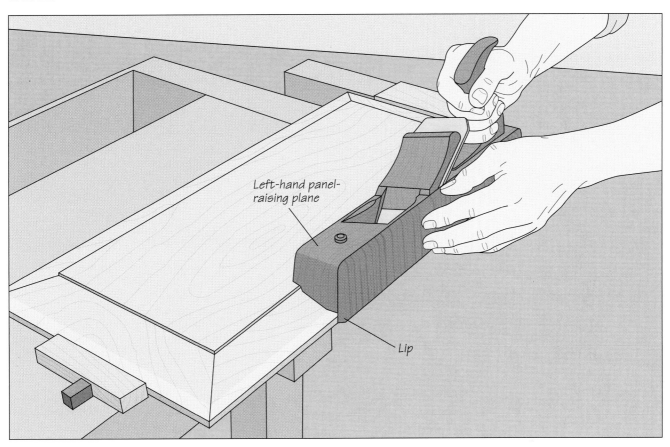

Left-hand panel-raising plane

Lip

Planing the bevels

With a matched pair of panel-raising planes—a right-hand tool and a left-hand model—you can bevel the edges of a panel. Cut the end grain first. Set the panel on a workbench, with the edge of the workpiece extending off the table and clamp it in place. Choose either the right- or left-hand plane so that the blade cuts with the grain. Set the cutting depth at no more than $1/32$ inch and make a few passes, guiding the plane along the surface with the tool's lip flush against the outer edge of the panel. Continue until the bevel has the desired profile. Reposition the panel and bevel the opposite end the same way using the other plane. Repeat the process to bevel the two remaining edges with the grain, using the right-handed plane to cut one edge and the left-hand tool for the opposite one (above).

SHOP TIP

Invisible nailer

To hide nails in cabinet work, use an invisible nailer, also known as a blind nailer. This

commercial device works like a miniature instrument maker's plane, using a $1/4$-inch chisel cutter to lift a thin wood shaving under which a nail can then be driven. The shaving can be glued right back down to conceal the nail. To use the nailer, adjust it following the manufacturer's instructions. The shaving is usually $1/32$-inch thick and long enough to enable you to comfortably drive a nail underneath. Practice on a piece of scrap first. Use a strip of masking tape to hold the shaving down while the glue is drying.

A SELECTION OF SHAPING TOOLS

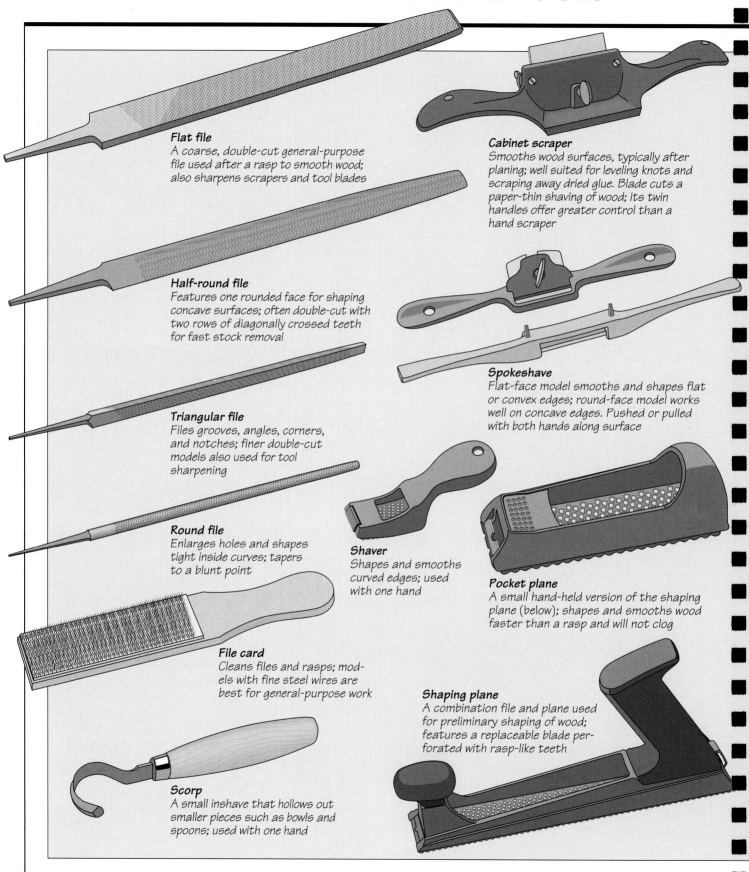

Flat file
A coarse, double-cut general-purpose file used after a rasp to smooth wood; also sharpens scrapers and tool blades

Half-round file
Features one rounded face for shaping concave surfaces; often double-cut with two rows of diagonally crossed teeth for fast stock removal

Triangular file
Files grooves, angles, corners, and notches; finer double-cut models also used for tool sharpening

Round file
Enlarges holes and shapes tight inside curves; tapers to a blunt point

File card
Cleans files and rasps; models with fine steel wires are best for general-purpose work

Scorp
A small inshave that hollows out smaller pieces such as bowls and spoons; used with one hand

Cabinet scraper
Smooths wood surfaces, typically after planing; well suited for leveling knots and scraping away dried glue. Blade cuts a paper-thin shaving of wood; its twin handles offer greater control than a hand scraper

Spokeshave
Flat-face model smooths and shapes flat or convex edges; round-face model works well on concave edges. Pushed or pulled with both hands along surface

Shaver
Shapes and smooths curved edges; used with one hand

Pocket plane
A small hand-held version of the shaping plane (below); shapes and smooths wood faster than a rasp and will not clog

Shaping plane
A combination file and plane used for preliminary shaping of wood; features a replaceable blade perforated with rasp-like teeth

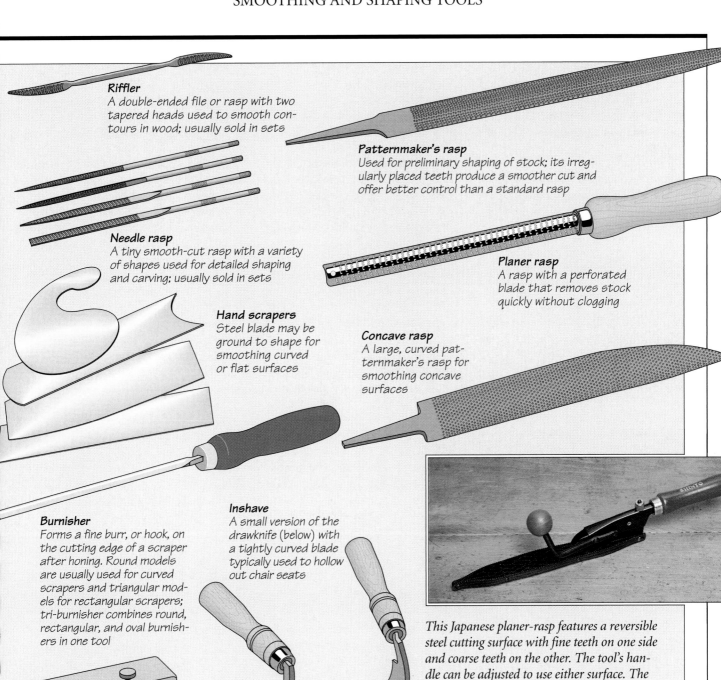

Riffler
A double-ended file or rasp with two tapered heads used to smooth contours in wood; usually sold in sets

Patternmaker's rasp
Used for preliminary shaping of stock; its irregularly placed teeth produce a smoother cut and offer better control than a standard rasp

Needle rasp
A tiny smooth-cut rasp with a variety of shapes used for detailed shaping and carving; usually sold in sets

Planer rasp
A rasp with a perforated blade that removes stock quickly without clogging

Hand scrapers
Steel blade may be ground to shape for smoothing curved or flat surfaces

Concave rasp
A large, curved patternmaker's rasp for smoothing concave surfaces

Burnisher
Forms a fine burr, or hook, on the cutting edge of a scraper after honing. Round models are usually used for curved scrapers and triangular models for rectangular scrapers; tri-burnisher combines round, rectangular, and oval burnishers in one tool

Inshave
A small version of the drawknife (below) with a tightly curved blade typically used to hollow out chair seats

This Japanese planer-rasp features a reversible steel cutting surface with fine teeth on one side and coarse teeth on the other. The tool's handle can be adjusted to use either surface. The tapered design allows access to tight spots.

Variable burnisher
A highly accurate, adjustable burnisher with a dial permitting selection of any hook angle between 0° and 15°

Drawknife
Shaves stock aggressively; also used to shape wood blanks prior to smoothing and shaping with plane and spokeshave. Blade is pulled

Between the drawknife, with its capacity to take large bites of wood, and the precision contouring tools known as rifflers, lie files and rasps, two common and frequently used shaping tools in the woodworker's toolbox.

Files and rasps are classified according to their shape, cut, and coarseness. There are flat files to smooth flat surfaces, round and half-round files for contoured surfaces, and triangular files for reaching into restricted spaces like corners and keyholes.

The cut of a file refers to the arrangement of its teeth. Single-cut files have one set of continuous, parallel teeth running across the face of the blade. These are often used for sharpening tool blades and scrapers. Double-cut files have a second set of teeth running across the first, forming a series of points, which makes for a rougher cut.

Although a double-cut file will cut wood quickly, the job is usually left to the rasp, which has large, individual teeth rather than a lined pattern of cutting edges. Rasp teeth shear slivers of wood with relative ease, but they leave a rough surface which must usually be smoothed with a file or sandpaper.

The coarseness of a file or a rasp depends on the depth of the teeth and the spacing between them. In order of increasing fineness, files are graded bastard, second, and smooth cuts. Smooth files have closely packed, shallow teeth. Rasps are available as bastard and second cuts. In general, the longer a rasp or file, the coarser its teeth will be. While any file can be used on wood, finer cuts clog quickly with shavings, making sandpaper a better choice for final smoothing of a work. A double-cut bastard file is your best bet for shaping tasks.

Grip the tool with both hands and work diagonally across the grain, applying even pressure. Since file teeth face away from the handle, they cut only on the push stroke. For that reason, you should avoid moving a file back and forth like a saw; this will dull the teeth. Instead, raise the teeth clear of the surface on the return stroke. For an extra-smooth result, hold the file with both hands perpendicular to the grain of the workpiece and draw the blade gently along the grain, guiding it back and forth.

Whenever you are filing, clamp the workpiece securely. If the file or rasp has no handle, fit it with one first; an exposed tang can be hazardous. Almost anything that suits you will do: Some woodworkers use old golf balls as makeshift handles. To help reduce clogging, sprinkle file or rasp teeth lightly with chalk. Oiling is not recommended as it attracts sawdust.

An inshave slices thin shavings from a flat, oval panel, transforming the surface into a chair seat.

SHOP TIP

Cleaning a file or rasp
The fine wood shavings produced by filing tend to stick to the tool and clog its teeth. This both reduces the blade's cutting efficiency and causes uneven scoring of the workpiece. To loosen dust and shavings from a file or rasp, use a file card. Start by lightly tapping the file on your bench to release some of the sawdust. Then draw the card's wire bristles across the blade, scrubbing parallel to the rows of teeth. For finer rasps or files, use a card with a brush. Pick out stubborn particles with a nail.

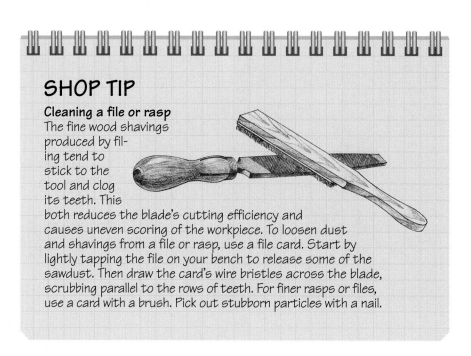

SHAPING DETAILS

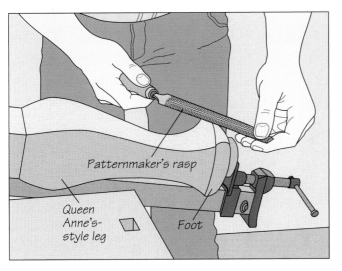

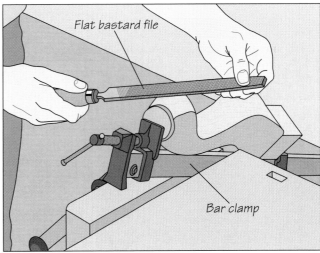

1 Shaping and smoothing the foot

Rasps, files, and rifflers work well in tandem for shaping and smoothing decorative details on contoured workpieces, like the foot on the Queen Anne-style leg shown in the illustrations on this page. Begin by securing the leg in a bar clamp and fixing the clamp in a vise. To shape the foot, use a patternmaker's rasp. Holding the rasp at an angle of about 45° to the leg, push the tool across the surface in overlapping passes until the desired contour begins to emerge *(above, left)*. Rotate the leg in the clamp as necessary so that you can shape the foot all the way around. Once the foot has the shape you want, smooth the wood using a double-cut flat bastard file. Work the surface as you did with the rasp *(above, right)*. Finish the job with sandpaper, using progressively finer-grit papers until the surface is smooth.

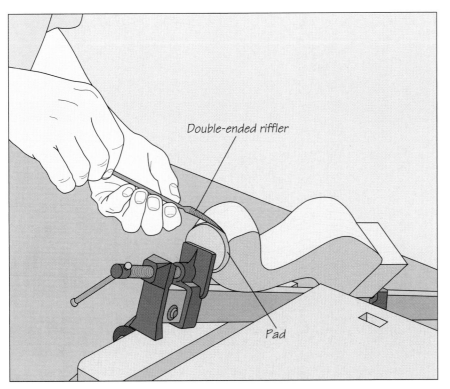

2 Shaping the pad

Use a tapered double-ended riffler to shape fine details, such as the pad under the foot. Holding the riffler with both hands, file around the base of the foot with the curved head of the tool. Continue until the pad is uniformly rounded *(left)*, rotating the leg in the clamp as necessary. Use a needle file or needle rasp to smooth the pad.

SMOOTHING EDGES

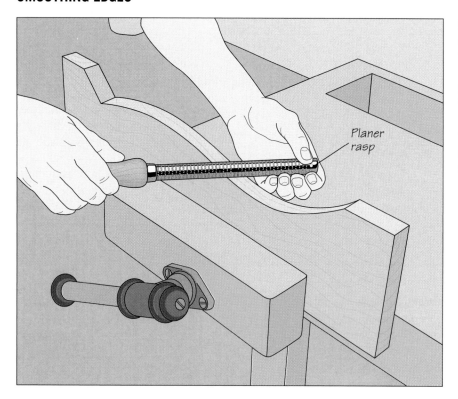

Planer rasp

Smoothing a saw cut

A planer rasp will give the final contour to a curved saw cut. Secure the workpiece in a vise. Holding the rasp with both hands so that its teeth are facing down, push the blade diagonally across the grain *(left)*. Use moderate pressure, working from one end of the surface to the other. Finish smoothing the wood with a round wood file.

Shaping and smoothing a contoured surface

To give a contoured workpiece such as a cabriole leg its finished shape, and smooth its surface, use a spokeshave. Secure the leg as shown on page 105. Pull the spokeshave slowly toward you with both hands, cutting a thin shaving that follows the grain *(right)*. Exert moderate pressure and keep your arms rigid. Continue until the contour you want begins to take shape and the surface is smooth, adjusting the angle of the tool after each stroke to follow the curved surface. If the grain direction changes partway through the stroke, causing the blade to chatter or skip, reverse your direction and push the spokeshave rather than pull it. Rotate the leg in the bar clamp to shape and smooth the other edges.

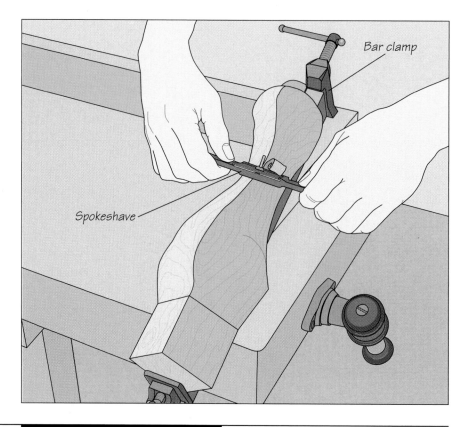

Bar clamp

Spokeshave

SCRAPING TECHNIQUES

Scraping is often overlooked, or viewed as an intermediate step between planing and sanding a wood surface. But there are several situations in which a well-sharpened and properly used scraper is a good alternative to a plane or an abrasive.

Planes can tear irregular or interlocking grain and sandpaper produces minute scratches. But a scraper severs wood fibers cleanly, leaving a smooth, even surface behind. The versatile tool can also flatten high spots, scrape away dried glue, and clean up torn edges.

The two most common versions are the hand scraper and the cabinet scraper. Available in a range of thicknesses and shapes for every scraping task, hand scrapers are single blades of spring steel honed to form a cutting edge. Unlike a plane blade, a scraper has a burr, or hook, turned along each side of its cutting edge. This allows the implement to be pulled or pushed in any direction, getting the cut-

ting edge into corners and tight spots a plane cannot reach. The cabinet scraper works much like the hand scraper, except that its blade is mounted in a metal body that resembles a spokeshave, providing greater control.

With a mere 1/32 inch of blade protruding from its body, a properly sharpened cabinet scraper can smooth a wood surface as effectively as the finest grit of sandpaper.

The cutting edges of scrapers dull quickly and require regular sharpening; most new scrapers also need to be sharpened before use. Sharpening a hand scraper is a three-step operation in which the existing hook is removed, the cutting edges are honed, and a new hook is formed. The size of the shaving a scraper produces will let you know when it is time to sharpen; the duller the blade, the smaller the shaving.

As its name implies, a scraper works by scraping, not cutting; its burr is dragged along the surface by holding the blade at a relatively flat angle. Held perpendicular, the blade will tend to gouge, dent, or scratch the surface. Held at more of an angle, the scraper will cut away less wood, but leave a smoother surface. To find the ideal angle for scraping, hold the scraper almost parallel to the work surface and begin scraping while gradually raising the angle of the blade until it produces the desired finish.

SHARPENING A HAND SCRAPER

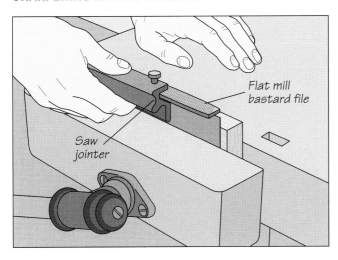

1 Filing the edges square
Secure the scraper in a vise, edge up, with a wood block on one side to keep it rigid. Clamp a mill bastard file in a commercial saw jointer and, holding the jointer firmly against one side of the scraper, exert moderate pressure as you make several passes back and forth along the edge of the tool *(above)* until the existing hook disappears and the edge is flat. Turn the scraper over in the vise and repeat the process for the other edge.

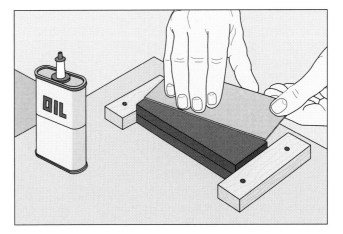

2 Honing the edges
Secure a combination sharpening stone fine side up to a work surface with cleats and lubricate it as you would to hone a plane blade *(page 83)*. Holding the scraper flat against the stone, rub each face on the stone with a circular motion *(above)* until any roughness produced by filing disappears. To complete the process, hold the scraper upright and slide the edges back and forth diagonally across the stone until they are smooth with sharp corners.

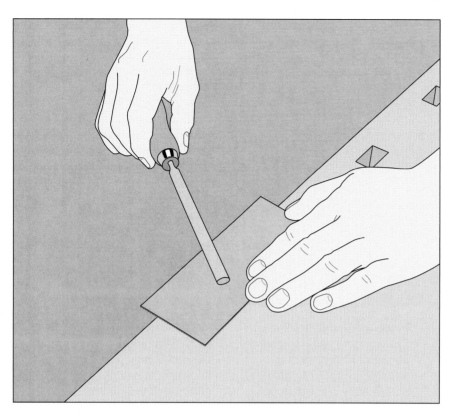

3 Burnishing the edges
Wipe a tiny amount of oil onto the edge of the scraper. Form a hook on each cutting edge of the scraper by laying the scraper flat on a work surface with an edge extending off the table, then run the burnisher back and forth along the edge *(left)*, exerting strong downward pressure. Burnish the other cutting edge the same way, then turn the scraper over and burnish the edges on the other face.

4 Completing the hook
Secure the scraper edge-up in the vise and wipe a little more oil onto its edge. Holding the burnisher level, make a few passes along the edge in one direction until the edge swells slightly. Apply moderate pressure to turn the edge outward on one side *(right)*. Then hold the burnisher so that the handle is 10° to 15° above the horizontal and continue burnishing until the edge turns over. To form a hook on the other side of the edge *(inset)*, repeat the process with the handle in your other hand. The greater the pressure you apply, the bigger the hook. Turn the scraper over in the vise and complete the hooks on the other edge.

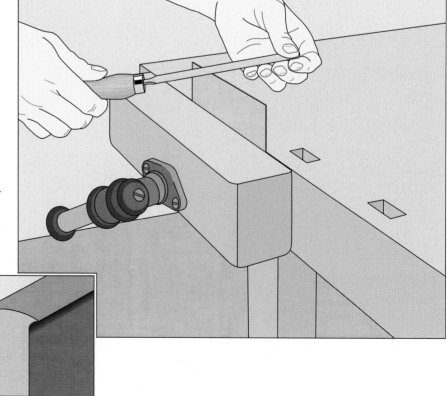

USING HAND SCRAPERS

Smoothing a flat surface

To smooth a flat surface, such as the rails and stiles of a frame-and-panel door, secure the workpiece so that you will be able to work with the wood grain. Standing at one end of the workpiece, curl your fingers around the front of the scraper and press on the back with your thumbs to bow the metal outward. Tilt the scraper forward at about 20° from the vertical and scrape the surface, moving toward the far end of the workpiece *(right)*. Scrape at a slight angle to the grain, applying moderate pressure with long, fluid strokes and lifting the scraper before stopping at the end of each stroke. You can also pull the scraper along the surface, but make sure the tool is bowed toward you. As you move to each new surface, reposition the workpiece so that you can always scrape with the grain.

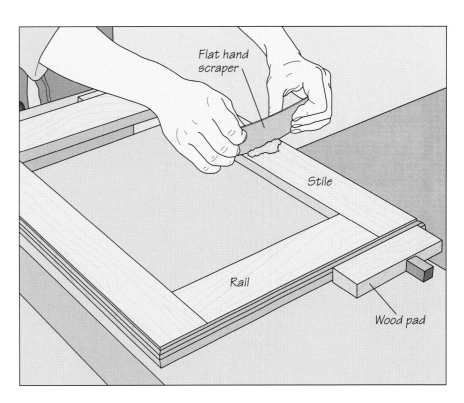

Flat hand scraper

Stile

Rail

Wood pad

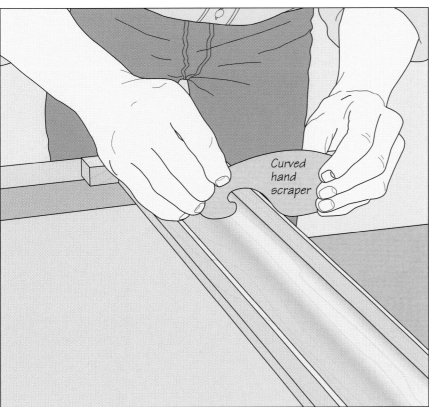

Curved hand scraper

Scraping a curved surface

A curved scraper is designed to smooth a convex or concave surface, such as a length of molding. Clamp the workpiece and position the tool so that its edge fits the surface. Curve the scraper slightly and scrape as you would a flat surface *(left)*.

STRIKING AND FASTENING TOOLS

The non-tapered tip of a cabinetmaker's screwdriver enables it to drive a screw into a counterbore hole without marring the sides of the hole.

The history of striking and fastening tools is as old as woodworking itself. The earliest hammers and mallets were little more than simple stone implements and heavy blocks of wood used to drive home nails, fit joints together, and disassemble furniture. Later, true hammers emerged, forged by hand by blacksmiths. The screwdriver, known as a turnscrew until the early 19th Century, was originally nothing more than a simple flat-tipped instrument limited to turning slotted-head screws. But as the following pages show, both tools have been refined over the years so that today there is a specific striking or fastening tool for every task.

Nevertheless, hammers and screwdrivers are among the most abused tools in the workshop. Craftsmen who would not dream of ripping a board and cutting dovetails with the same saw, or smoothing end grain and flat surfaces with a single plane, laboriously use the same claw hammer to drive brads, finishing nails and larger nails, and tap joints in place. Screwdrivers, too, suffer from the tendency of otherwise well-equipped cabinetmakers to "make do" with one or two sizes, which may be called upon to do the work of pry bars and chisels. In every case, the tool and its user end up doing many jobs poorly and few tasks well.

Each of the striking and fastening tools shown in this chapter has a specific application. The cabinetmaker's hammer, for example, has two faces: One is specially designed to start brads and small finishing nails, while the other drives them home *(page 112)*. Dead-blow hammers are ideal for assembling and disassembling joints, while wooden mallets are the best tools for striking chisels and gouges. And no woodworking shop is complete without a proper assortment of screwdrivers.

The right tool should be of good quality. Look for cross-ground screwdriver tips, or tips that have been ground horizontally, rather than vertically. This feature makes the sides of the tips more abrasive and less glossy, giving them a better grip on screw heads. Some are even available with horizontal grooves running across the tips for an improved hold on screws.

Technology has improved even the simplest tools. The claw hammer has undergone subtle but significant modification. Better steel and forging processes have created tough, hard heads. High-tech plastic, reinforced with carbon and glass fibers, makes nearly indestructible handles. Few such changes have affected the wooden mallet, however. Lignum vitae is probably the best choice for a mallet, but there are many worthy substitutes, including European beech, maple, and oak..

A wooden carpenter's mallet taps a pair of dowels into a tapered leg, which will then be attached to a rail with matching holes.

A SELECTION OF HAMMERS AND MALLETS

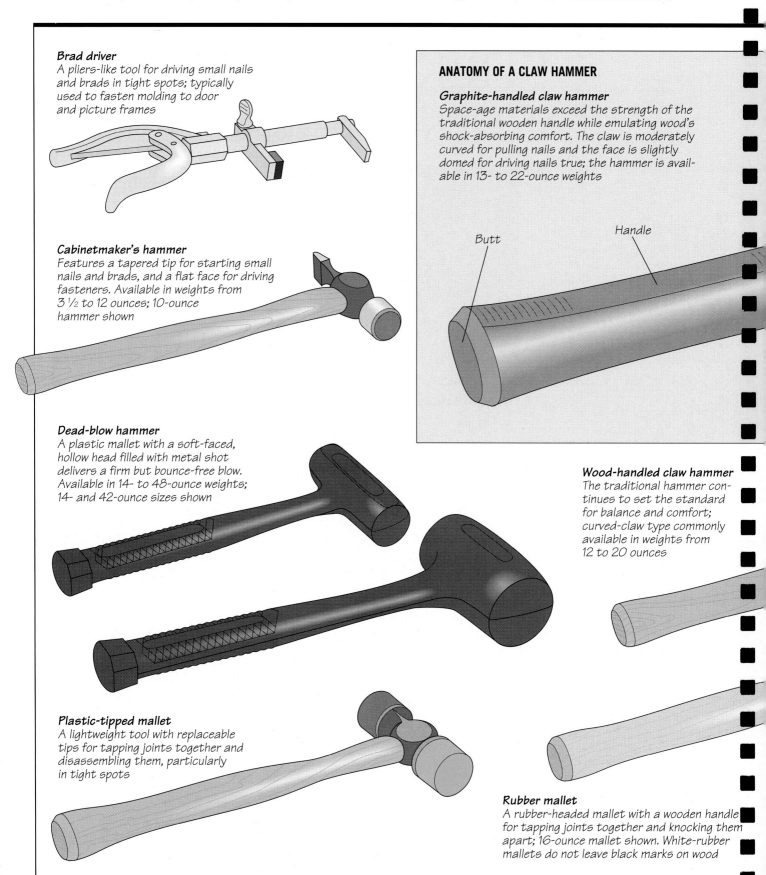

Brad driver
A pliers-like tool for driving small nails and brads in tight spots; typically used to fasten molding to door and picture frames

Cabinetmaker's hammer
Features a tapered tip for starting small nails and brads, and a flat face for driving fasteners. Available in weights from 3 1/2 to 12 ounces; 10-ounce hammer shown

Dead-blow hammer
A plastic mallet with a soft-faced, hollow head filled with metal shot delivers a firm but bounce-free blow. Available in 14- to 48-ounce weights; 14- and 42-ounce sizes shown

Plastic-tipped mallet
A lightweight tool with replaceable tips for tapping joints together and disassembling them, particularly in tight spots

ANATOMY OF A CLAW HAMMER

Graphite-handled claw hammer
Space-age materials exceed the strength of the traditional wooden handle while emulating wood's shock-absorbing comfort. The claw is moderately curved for pulling nails and the face is slightly domed for driving nails true; the hammer is available in 13- to 22-ounce weights

Butt

Handle

Wood-handled claw hammer
The traditional hammer continues to set the standard for balance and comfort; curved-claw type commonly available in weights from 12 to 20 ounces

Rubber mallet
A rubber-headed mallet with a wooden handle for tapping joints together and knocking them apart; 16-ounce mallet shown. White-rubber mallets do not leave black marks on wood

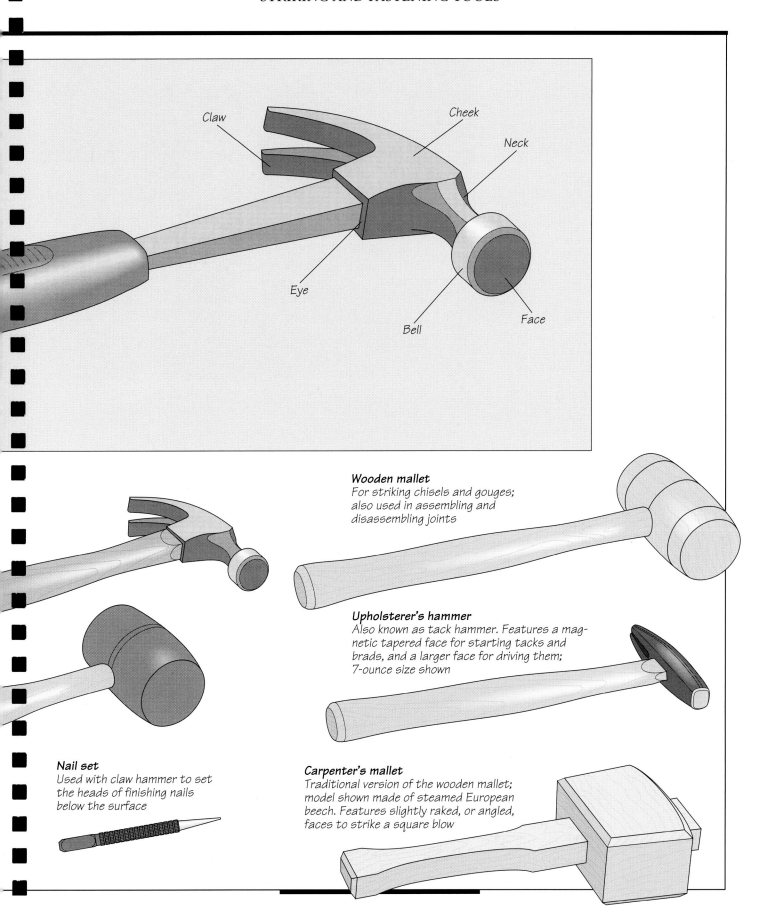

Claw

Cheek

Neck

Eye

Bell

Face

Wooden mallet
For striking chisels and gouges; also used in assembling and disassembling joints

Upholsterer's hammer
Also known as tack hammer. Features a magnetic tapered face for starting tacks and brads, and a larger face for driving them; 7-ounce size shown

Nail set
Used with claw hammer to set the heads of finishing nails below the surface

Carpenter's mallet
Traditional version of the wooden mallet; model shown made of steamed European beech. Features slightly raked, or angled, faces to strike a square blow

HAMMERS AND MALLETS

Hammers are simple tools that make driving nails seem the easiest of tasks. And while it is true that pounding nails into a board scarcely seems to require instruction, even this most basic activity can benefit from the use of proper technique and a few tricks of the trade. Acquired skill and extra care will enable you to sink a row of finishing nails into a fine cabinet without marring the surface.

For best results, use a well-balanced hammer with a forged head; the cast heads used on low-cost models tend to mushroom and shatter with use. The best hammers feature a slightly convex face, allowing nails to be driven flush without leaving hammer marks on the surface. Placing a piece of perforated hardboard between the hammer head and the wood and then using a nail set to sink nail heads below the surface offers an additional measure of protection.

Consider the force you use. A short swing from the wrist is sufficient to drive finishing nails, but a fuller swing, involving elbow and shoulder action, should be used with larger nails.

Nails that bend or go askew as you drive them should be removed, not straightened in place. To pull a nail, place a small wood block under the hammer head to provide extra leverage and to protect the surface. Before nailing into dense hardwoods or an obstruction like a knot, bore a pilot hole.

Some safety reminders: Wear safety glasses and do not use a damaged hammer or one with a loose handle. Never strike one hammer head against another; the heads may shatter. Use the face of the hammer to strike a nail, rather than the cheek. Keep hammer and mallet faces free of oil and dirt.

A dead-blow hammer strikes a chair leg to separate it from the leg rails. The metal shot in the head absorbs the blow, focusing the impact on the leg and preventing the hammer from rebounding.

SHOP TIP

Choosing a durable hammer
Despite the availability of a variety of man-made compounds such as graphite and fiberglass, wooden-handled hammers remain a popular choice among craftsmen. They are light yet strong and feature a well-balanced feel. The strength of wooden handles varies greatly, however, depending on the orientation of their wood grain to the hammer head. Choose a hammer with a handle that has the grain running perpendicular to the face; handles with grain parallel to the face tend to break more easily.

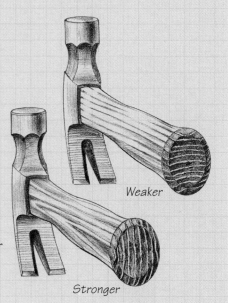

Weaker

Stronger

DRIVING NAILS

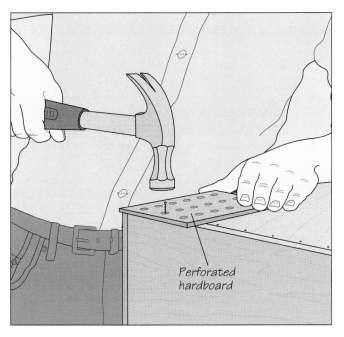
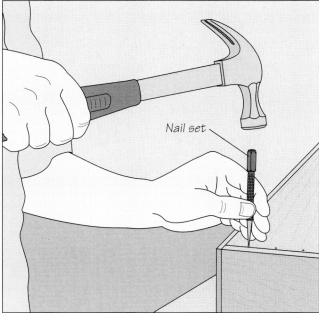

Perforated hardboard

Nail set

Using a claw hammer

To protect the workpiece, slip a piece of perforated hardboard over the nail head once the nail has been started. Holding the hammer near the butt of the handle, drive the nail with short strokes *(above, left)*. To set the nail head flush with or slightly below the surface, use a nail set with a tip the same size as the nail head. Place the nail set on the center of the nail head and tap it sharply with the hammer *(above, right)*. To conceal a nail head you have driven below the surface, cover it by rubbing with a wax stick.

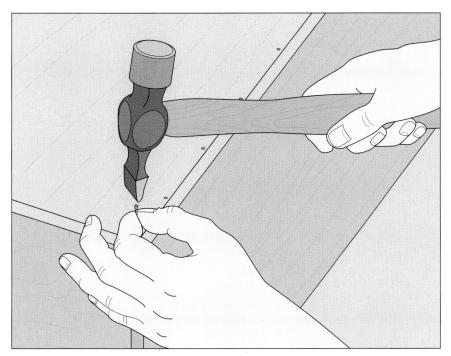

Using a cabinetmaker's hammer

Use a cabinetmaker's hammer to drive small nails and tacks. To start a nail, hold it between your thumb and index finger, and tap it lightly with the tapered end of the hammer *(left)*. Alternatively, you can start a very small nail by holding it upright in a piece of cardboard with a slot cut into it. Once the nail has been started, drive it home as you would with a claw hammer.

REPLACING A HAMMER HANDLE

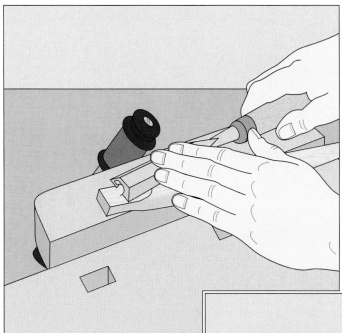

1 Removing the old handle and preparing the new one
A split, splintered or broken wooden hammer handle can easily be replaced, making a timeworn tool as good as new. To remove the old handle, saw it off just below the head and tap out the wood remaining in the head with a chisel or a punch. If the wood is difficult to remove, bore a few holes through it. To prepare the replacement handle, secure it in a vise and pare it to fit into the head using a chisel *(left)*. For best results, use a slicing motion toward the top of the handle; periodically test-fit the head until it slides on snugly. Then clamp the handle upright in the vise and saw a kerf into it as deep as the length of the wedge you will use in step 3. Make the kerf perpendicular to the orientation of the head.

2 Attaching the head
Fit the head on the new handle and tap the butt on a work surface to allow the weight of the head to settle it on the handle *(near right)*. To finish fastening the head, hold the hammer head-down with one hand and strike the butt repeatedly with a wooden mallet *(far right)*. If the handle emerges from the top of the head, saw it off flush.

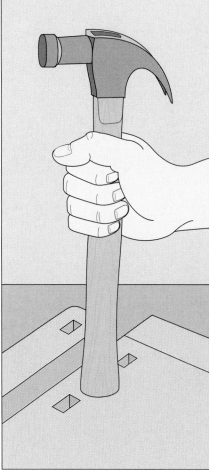

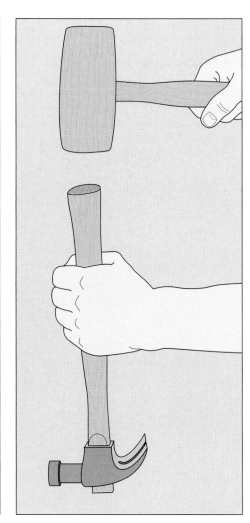

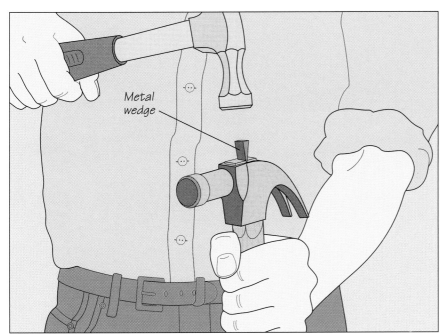

Metal wedge

3 Inserting a wedge

Insert a commercial metal hammer-wedge into the kerf you cut in step 1 and tap it into the handle until the wedge is flush with the top. Make sure the wedge goes in straight; tap it occasionally on the side to straighten it out, if necessary.

BUILD IT YOURSELF

A WOODEN MALLET

Shop-building your own wooden mallet from laminated pieces of hardwood is an inexpensive way to stock your shop with a selection of these useful, durable tools. Although the illustration includes suggested dimensions, you can size the mallet to suit your needs.

Cut the three head blanks and the handle from a wood like oak or maple. To fashion the handle, taper the sides slightly from both ends to the middle on the band saw. Then saw a kerf into one end of the handle. Copy the handle's shape onto the middle head blank and saw it out. Then glue up the mallet, alternating the grain direction of the head pieces to provide the maximum strength.

Allow the glue to dry overnight; once it has cured, insert a shop-made wooden wedge in the kerf and tap it in place, then shape the head to your liking on the band saw. Mallet heads are typically rounded on the top with slight angles on each face to ensure square striking. Chamfer the edges of the head to prevent it from splitting and cut a bevel along the edges of the handle for a comfortable grip.

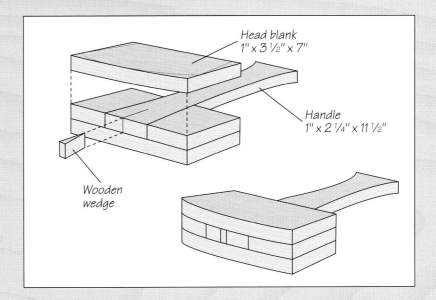

Head blank
1" x 3 1/2" x 7"

Handle
1" x 2 1/4" x 11 1/2"

Wooden wedge

A GALLERY OF SCREWDRIVERS

Screwdrivers are frequently sold in sets with a variety of tip sizes and shank lengths. Flat-tip screwdrivers are available in an infinite number of tip sizes, while Phillips and square drive (or Robertson) models are limited to four. Shank lengths vary from stubby to extralong. Many handle styles are also available, but the most common is fluted plastic molded directly onto the shaft. Screwdrivers often feature flat, square, or hex-shaped shanks that enable a wrench to be used when additional torque is required.

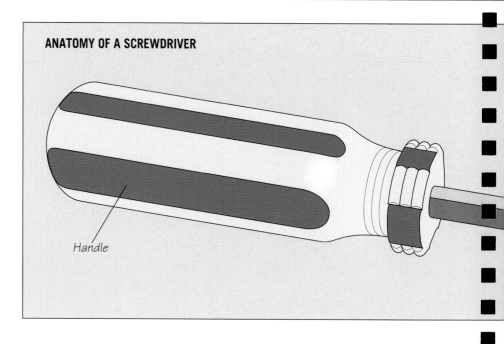

ANATOMY OF A SCREWDRIVER

Handle

Offset screwdriver
Also known as cranked screwdriver; turns screws in restricted spaces. Available with flat or Phillips tips, or one of each, in various sizes

Offset ratchet screwdriver
Offset screwdriver with reversible ratchet mechanism

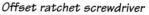

Jeweler's screwdriver
Used for turning tiny screws, especially in restricted spaces; typically available in sets which include flat, Phillips, and awl-shaped tips

Spiral ratchet screwdriver
Similar to ratchet screwdriver; tip turns when handle is pushed in. Depending on setting, drives or removes screws, or works as a standard or ratchet driver

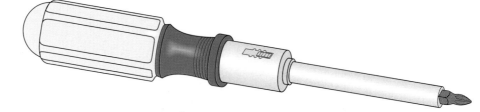

Magnetizer/ demagnetizer
Magnetizes the tips of screwdrivers to hold steel screws

Ratchet screwdriver
The handle's ratchet mechanism permits fast turning of screws; typically available with interchangeable flat, Phillips, and Robertson tips that can be stored in the handle

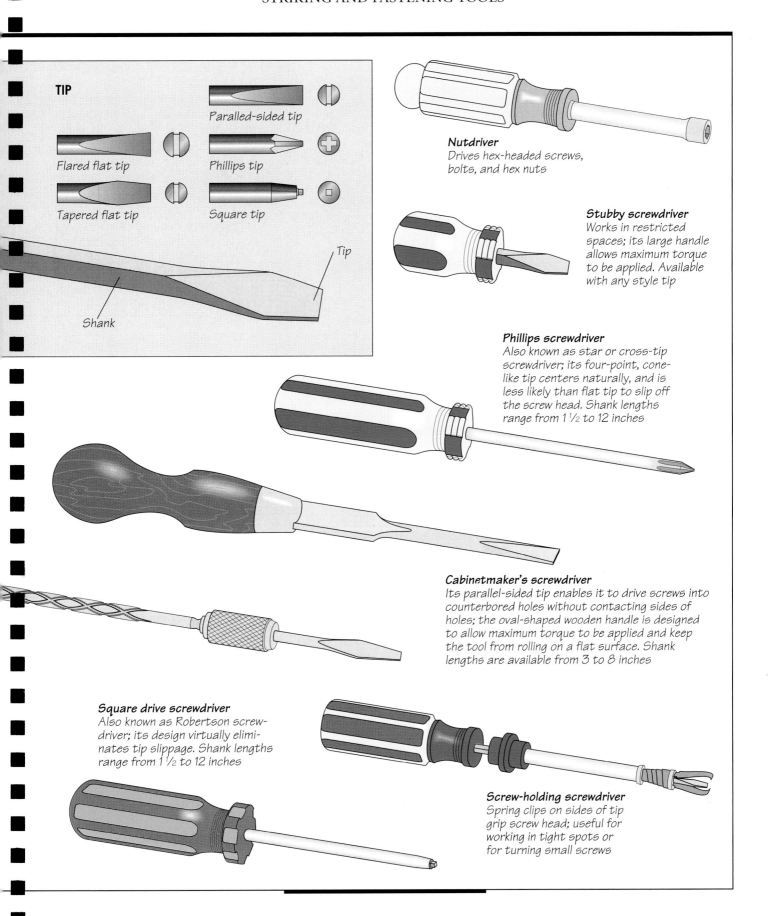

TIP

Flared flat tip

Paralled-sided tip

Tapered flat tip

Phillips tip

Square tip

Tip

Shank

Nutdriver
Drives hex-headed screws, bolts, and hex nuts

Stubby screwdriver
Works in restricted spaces; its large handle allows maximum torque to be applied. Available with any style tip

Phillips screwdriver
Also known as star or cross-tip screwdriver; its four-point, cone-like tip centers naturally, and is less likely than flat tip to slip off the screw head. Shank lengths range from 1 ½ to 12 inches

Cabinetmaker's screwdriver
Its parallel-sided tip enables it to drive screws into counterbored holes without contacting sides of holes; the oval-shaped wooden handle is designed to allow maximum torque to be applied and keep the tool from rolling on a flat surface. Shank lengths are available from 3 to 8 inches

Square drive screwdriver
Also known as Robertson screw-driver; its design virtually elimi-nates tip slippage. Shank lengths range from 1 ½ to 12 inches

Screw-holding screwdriver
Spring clips on sides of tip grip screw head; useful for working in tight spots or for turning small screws

SCREWDRIVERS

Try to match the screwdriver tip as closely as possible to the size of the screw head. This will reduce the chances of slippage which can mar a workpiece or cause a screwdriver tip to break. Avoid the temptation to use a damaged screwdriver. A flat-tip driver with a rounded or chipped tip, for example, is likely to slip off. In many cases, a damaged tip can be squared easily with a grinder *(page 121)*.

A long-handled screwdriver or one with a thicker handle will provide extra twisting power. To apply maximum torque, select a ratchet driver.

Before driving a screw into any dense wood you should predrill a hole to prevent the screw head from breaking off or the workpiece from splitting. Depending on how deep you wish to drive the screw, you may have to bore up to three overlapping holes of different diameters, one inside the next. Begin by marking

A ratchet screwdriver is ideal for turning screws where space is limited, such as inside the door opening of a cabinet.

the screw's location with an awl. To set the screw head on the surface of the wood, bore a pilot hole for the threads and a clearance hole for the shank. For maximum grip, the pilot hole should be slightly smaller than the screw threads; its depth should be about one-half the screw length in softwood, and about as deep as the screw length in hardwood. If you want the screw head to sit flush with the surface, bore a countersinking hole; to conceal the screw under a wood plug, bore a counterbore hole. You can bore these holes with a brace and bit or hand drill and a hand countersinker *(page 76)* or with an electric drill.

Where there is enough room for you to work with both hands, hold a screw steady in its hole while you start it. In tight spots, use a screw-holding screwdriver or magnetize the driver tip, as shown below.

DRIVING SCREWS IN RESTRICTED SPACES

Using a screw-holding screwdriver
Slide the collar on the shaft of the screwdriver toward the tip to open the screwholding clips. Fit the tip into the screw head slot and release the collar; the clips will close and grip the screw. Start the screw in the hole, then open the clips and drive the screw as you would with a standard tool *(right)*. To magnetize the shank of a standard screwdriver, use a commercial magnetizer/demagnetizer. Push the driver tip into the hole in the device and slide the magnetizer up and down on the shank a few times *(inset)*. The tip will be able to hold a steel screw. To demagnetize the screwdriver shank, slide it in the slot on the side of the device.

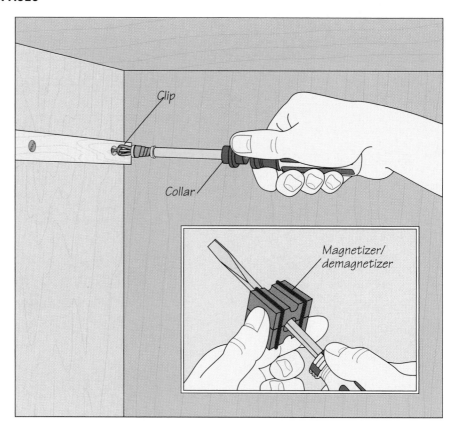

SALVAGING A DAMAGED SCREWDRIVER TIP

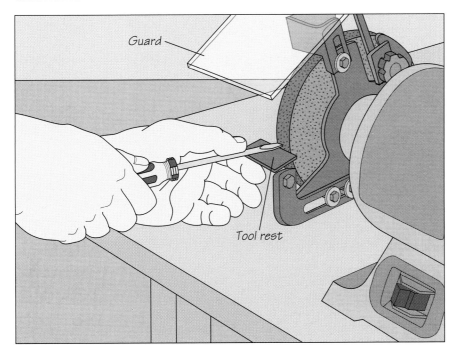

Guard

Tool rest

Squaring a screwdriver tip
Repair the tip of a flat-tip screwdriver on a grinder with a rough wheel. With the guard properly positioned and the tip clear of the wheel, switch on the machine. Holding the shaft between the index finger and thumb of one hand, set it on the grinder's tool rest and advance it toward the wheel until your index finger contacts the tool rest *(left)*. Slide the tip side-to-side across the wheel, pressing lightly while keeping your finger on the tool rest. The tip should remain perpendicular to the wheel throughout the operation. Check the tip regularly, stopping when it is square. Avoid overheating the tip, or it will turn blue—a sign it has lost its temper.

BUILD IT YOURSELF

A WALL-MOUNTED SCREWDRIVER RACK
To save time searching for the right screwdriver, store your collection in a shop-made wall rack. Bore a series of holes the size of the screwdriver shanks in a block of wood. To avoid sharp edges, round the corners of the rack.

To mount the rack on a wall, locate the studs behind it. Position the rack on the wall and mark the stud locations on one edge. Then drill a counterbore hole into the rack at each mark and a pilot hole through the wall into the studs. Screw the rack in place, making sure your fasteners are long enough to reach the studs.

Another option to attaching the rack to studs is to mount it to the wall with metal L-brackets and plastic anchors.

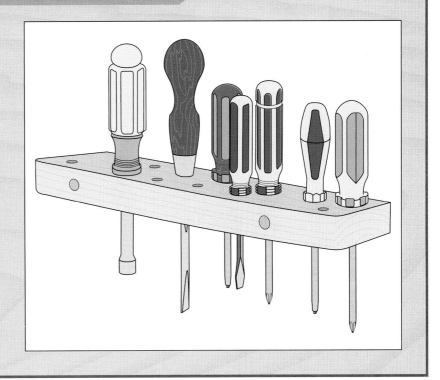

CLAMPS

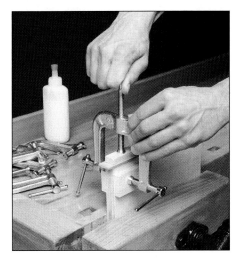

With its two outside screws gripping the opposite faces of a workpiece, the center screw of a three-way C clamp presses a length of edge banding in place during glue up.

Clamps may be the busiest tools in the woodworking shop. They are certainly the most numerous; some craftsmen line their shop walls with as many as three dozen clamps. And no wonder, because clamps are employed at almost every step of every project, from rough-out to final glue up.

There are clamps for every occasion, large and small, simple and versatile—like the ubiquitous C clamp—and complex and specialized, like the precision corner clamp. Many woodworkers adhere to the belief that they can never own enough clamps. Experience has proven them right more often than not. Hence, experts advise that an adequate startup set include what appears to a novice to be an astonishing number of clamps: several 4- and 6-inch C clamps, a pair of 8-inch wooden handscrews, several spring clamps, a half-dozen 4-foot pipe or bar clamps, and a web clamp.

Although you can buy all the clamps you need, you can make a surprising number of equally capable substitutes in your own shop, using such common materials as scrap wood, bicycle inner tubes, and rope. This chapter discusses the use of most types of clamps, and shows you how to make many devices yourself.

The two types of clamps that most woodworkers inevitably wish they had more of are trigger clamps and bar clamps. Trigger clamps are highly prized because they can handle a wide range of small- to medium-sized tasks. They are very powerful, have a relatively deep throat, and work one-handed.

Long-reaching bar and pipe clamps are indispensable for building large cabinets, assembling table frames and edge gluing boards into panels. They also provide a convenient way to dry-assemble cabinets prior to final glue up, which allows you to confirm that all the joints fit together snugly.

You can buy threaded couplings that allow you to join lengths of pipe together to create clamps of virtually any length.

A number of specialty clamps are available for tackling specific tasks. One of the most popular is the corner clamp. Designed to hold two workpieces together at an angle of 90°, this clamp is invaluable for gluing up drawers and other small carcases, especially those assembled with bevel joints. Other popular specialty clamps include picture frame clamps and three-way C clamps, which are used mainly to hold edge banding to shelving.

Like all other tools, clamps work best when guided by good technique. Often, all that is needed is the placement of blocks or strips of wood to protect surfaces and distribute their pressure. Most common techniques are described in the following pages.

A corner clamp holds the adjoining pieces of a miter joint at 90°. Applied on each of the corners of a picture frame, these clamps will produce a perfectly square frame.

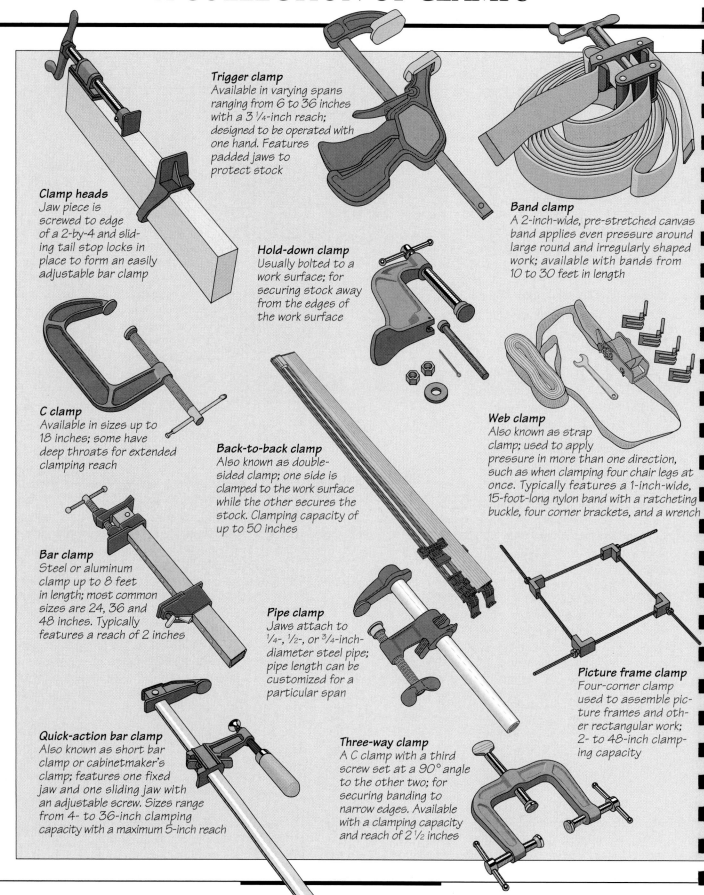

Trigger clamp
Available in varying spans ranging from 6 to 36 inches with a 3 1/4-inch reach; designed to be operated with one hand. Features padded jaws to protect stock

Clamp heads
Jaw piece is screwed to edge of a 2-by-4 and sliding tail stop locks in place to form an easily adjustable bar clamp

Hold-down clamp
Usually bolted to a work surface; for securing stock away from the edges of the work surface

Band clamp
A 2-inch-wide, pre-stretched canvas band applies even pressure around large round and irregularly shaped work; available with bands from 10 to 30 feet in length

C clamp
Available in sizes up to 18 inches; some have deep throats for extended clamping reach

Back-to-back clamp
Also known as double-sided clamp; one side is clamped to the work surface while the other secures the stock. Clamping capacity of up to 50 inches

Web clamp
Also known as strap clamp; used to apply pressure in more than one direction, such as when clamping four chair legs at once. Typically features a 1-inch-wide, 15-foot-long nylon band with a ratcheting buckle, four corner brackets, and a wrench

Bar clamp
Steel or aluminum clamp up to 8 feet in length; most common sizes are 24, 36 and 48 inches. Typically features a reach of 2 inches

Pipe clamp
Jaws attach to 1/4-, 1/2-, or 3/4-inch-diameter steel pipe; pipe length can be customized for a particular span

Picture frame clamp
Four-corner clamp used to assemble picture frames and other rectangular work; 2- to 48-inch clamping capacity

Quick-action bar clamp
Also known as short bar clamp or cabinetmaker's clamp; features one fixed jaw and one sliding jaw with an adjustable screw. Sizes range from 4- to 36-inch clamping capacity with a maximum 5-inch reach

Three-way clamp
A C clamp with a third screw set at a 90° angle to the other two; for securing banding to narrow edges. Available with a clamping capacity and reach of 2 1/2 inches

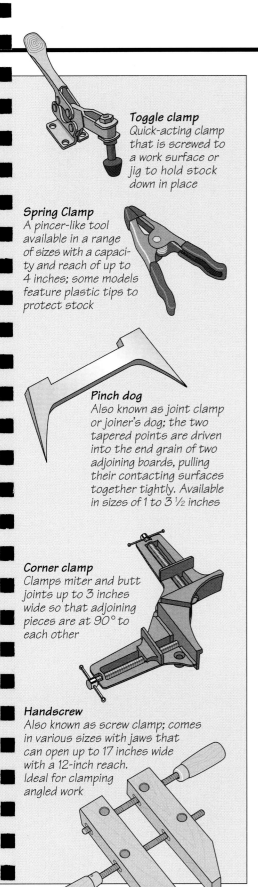

Toggle clamp
Quick-acting clamp that is screwed to a work surface or jig to hold stock down in place

Spring Clamp
A pincer-like tool available in a range of sizes with a capacity and reach of up to 4 inches; some models feature plastic tips to protect stock

Pinch dog
Also known as joint clamp or joiner's dog; the two tapered points are driven into the end grain of two adjoining boards, pulling their contacting surfaces together tightly. Available in sizes of 1 to 3 ½ inches

Corner clamp
Clamps miter and butt joints up to 3 inches wide so that adjoining pieces are at 90° to each other

Handscrew
Also known as screw clamp; comes in various sizes with jaws that can open up to 17 inches wide with a 12-inch reach. Ideal for clamping angled work

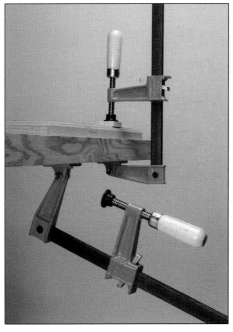

Hinged bar clamps resemble quick-action clamps with a pivoting head instead of a fixed jaw at one end. Fastened to the underside of a work surface, the pivoting head keeps the clamp out of the way when it is not in use, but allows it to swing up into position to secure work to top of the table. The clamps can also be attached to a track fixed under a table so that they can be slid to any position along the table's length.

CLAMPING ACCESSORIES

Rubber pads
Slip on jaws of bar, pipe, and C clamps to prevent marring stock

Center pipe clamp fixture
Fits on pipe section of pipe clamp to apply downward pressure

Pipe saddles
Brackets are screwed to a work surface and used to hold pipe clamps level and prevent them from falling over

Edge clamp fixture
Fitted onto the bar of a trigger clamp to apply clamping pressure at a 90° angle to the jaws

GLUING UP

Whether you are bonding boards together face-to-face to form a leg blank or edge-to-edge for a panel, there are certain principles that apply to most glue up operations. First, make sure that the contacting surfaces have been smoothed and squared on the jointer. The boards should appear to be a single piece of wood rather than a composite. Experiment with the boards in different configurations to produce a pattern that is visually interesting, but make sure that the grain runs in the same direction on all of the pieces. To minimize warping, arrange the boards so that the end grain of adjacent pieces runs in opposite directions, as shown below. When edge or face gluing, spread glue on one mating surface. To avoid marring the stock when you tighten the clamps, place wood pads between the clamp jaws and the work, or slip protective pads over the jaws.

The type of clamp you select for a particular operation depends on the clamping capacity and pressure you need. Use C clamps for face gluing and bar or pipe clamps for edge gluing. Avoid overtightening clamps when gluing up. This will squeeze out the glue and starve a joint of adhesive.

Fastened to a shop wall, a vertical glue press offers a convenient method of edge gluing boards while taking up much less space than a conventional glue table. The boards to be glued together are stacked edge to edge in the press, with the bottommost piece positioned on a metal support. When the hand wheels at the top of the press are tightened, the boards are pressed together snugly and the vertical bars are pulled inward, holding the boards in lateral alignment.

FACE GLUING

Clamping boards face-to-face

Although the three boards shown at right could be glued with the use of only four clamps, more clamps will distribute the pressure more evenly, resulting in a superior bond. The use of eight C clamps produces nearly constant force across the entire joint. Starting 1 or 2 inches from the ends of the boards, space the clamps at 3- to 4-inch intervals. Alternate the handle direction to provide more room to tighten the jaws. Tighten the clamps just enough to hold the contacting surfaces together, and position wood pads close to the top edge of the outside boards so that the clamping pressure is focused on the top half of the assembly. Turn the assembly over so that the first row of clamps is resting on the work surface and install the second row along the other edge *(right)*. Finish tightening all of the clamps until there are no gaps between the boards and a thin bead of glue squeezes out of the joints.

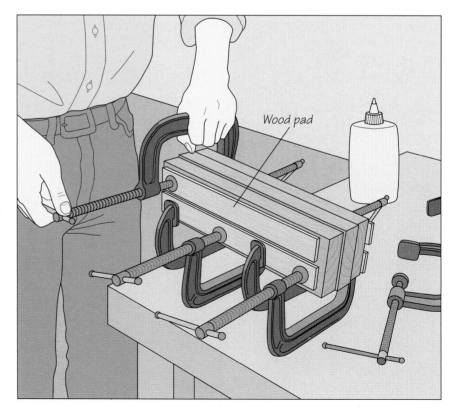

Wood pad

GLUING DOWN TRIM

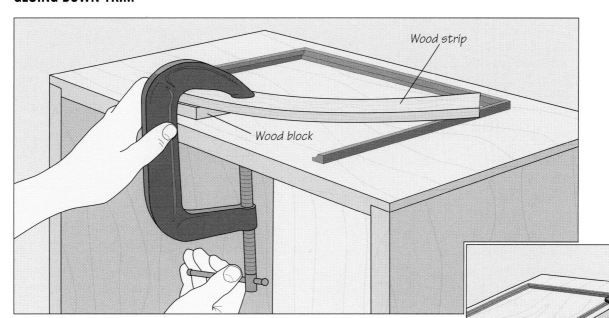

Wood strip

Wood block

Spring clamp

Using a C clamp
To increase the reach of a C clamp when you need to apply clamping pressure away from the edges of a work surface, use a wood strip as a clamp extension. Once the trim has been positioned, place a wood block of the same thickness as the trim near the edge of the surface and a wood strip long enough to reach from the block to the point on the trim where pressure is required. Install the C clamp on the strip just ahead of the wood block and tighten the clamp *(above)* until the far end of the strip is securely holding the piece of trim.

Using spring clamps
Spring clamps are intended to apply clamping pressure close to the edge of a work surface quickly and easily. Set the trim in place, then install the clamps so that the jaws sit squarely on the wood *(above)*; cover the jaws with protective rubber or plastic pads, if necessary. Use as many clamps as necessary to apply even pressure along the full length of the trim.

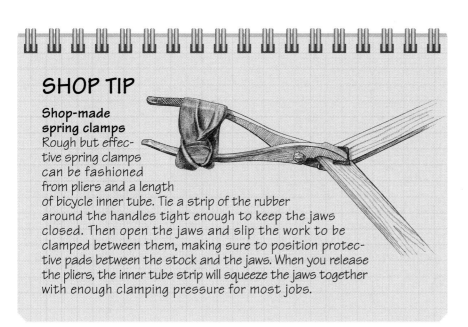

SHOP TIP

Shop-made spring clamps
Rough but effective spring clamps can be fashioned from pliers and a length of bicycle inner tube. Tie a strip of the rubber around the handles tight enough to keep the jaws closed. Then open the jaws and slip the work to be clamped between them, making sure to position protective pads between the stock and the jaws. When you release the pliers, the inner tube strip will squeeze the jaws together with enough clamping pressure for most jobs.

EDGE GLUING

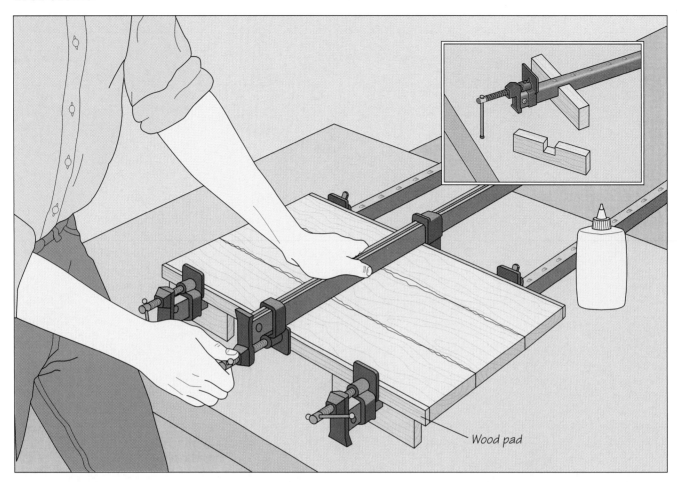

Wood pad

SHOP TIP

**Protective pads
for C clamps**
Instead of buying protective
pads for your clamps, you can
make your own inexpensively.
Film canister caps *(near
right)* will fit the jaws of most
C clamps. You can also use
felt *(middle right)* or a piece of
scrap wood *(far right)* cut to the proper size. In either case, clamping pressure will hold the pads in place.

Using bar clamps
Set as many bar clamps on a work surface as necessary to support the boards
to be glued at 24- to 36-inch intervals.
To keep the bars from moving, place
them in notched wood blocks *(inset)*.
Cut two pieces of scrap wood at least
as long as the boards and use them
as pads. With the boards set on edge
on the clamps, apply adhesive to their
contacting surfaces. Then set the boards
face down and line up their ends. Tighten
the clamps only enough to butt the
boards. Overtightening will make them
buckle up at the joints. Place additional clamps across the top of the
boards, centering them between each
pair below. Tighten the clamps after
they are all in place *(above)*.

BUILD IT YOURSELF

CROSSBARS FOR EDGE GLUING

To keep panels from bowing when clamping pressure is applied during glue up, place a pair of shop-made crossbars between each pair of bar clamps. Make each crossbar from two short wood spacers and two strips of 1-by-1 stock a few inches longer than the panel's width. The spacers should be slightly thicker than the diameter of the bolts used to hold the crossbars to the panel. Glue the spacers between the ends of the strips. Install the crossbars in pairs after all the bar clamps have been tightened, centering them between the clamps already in place. Use machine bolts with washers and wing nuts to hold the crossbars snug against the panel *(right)*. Wax the bars to prevent excess glue from adhering.

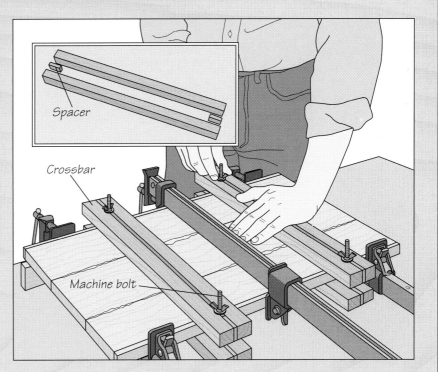

Spacer

Crossbar

Machine bolt

SHOP TIP

Edge gluing thin stock

The edge gluing method shown here was developed by guitar makers to overcome a particular problem: Edge gluing thin stock with bar clamps risks buckling the boards when the clamps are tightened. Place the boards to be joined on wooden bars that are a few inches longer than the width of the panel. Spread glue on the contacting surfaces, then tie a loop at one end of a length of rope and fit it around the end of one of the strips. Weave the rope over the boards and under the bars before making it fast with a knot. Repeat the process with the other wood strip and tighten the ropes by driving wooden wedges between them and the top of the panel. Wax the bearing surfaces of the wedges and bars to prevent them from being glued to the panel.

GLUING UP EXTRA-WIDE PANELS

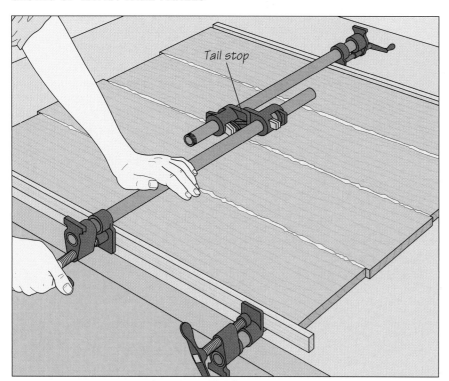

Tail stop

Using pipe clamps in pairs
If you lack enough long pipe clamps to glue an extra-wide panel, double up two shorter clamps to function as a single long one. Set up the boards to be joined as you would for a panel of standard width. To fashion a long clamp, position two shorter clamps across the panel so that the handle-end jaws rest against opposite edges and the tail stops of the clamps overlap. Tighten one of the clamps until the tail stops make contact *(left)*. As you continue to tighten the clamp, it will pull the boards together in the same manner as a single long clamp. Use string to tie the clamps together and keep them from slipping apart.

BUILD IT YOURSELF

PIPE CLAMP EXTENDER
The shop-built jig shown at right will extend the capacity of your pipe clamps. Cut the main body of the extender from 1-by-6 stock and the cleat from a 2-by-2. Saw a D-shaped cutout near one end of the body to accommodate the pipe clamp tail stop, then screw the cleat to the body *(inset)*.

To use the jig, set the cleat against one edge of the workpiece to be glued up and fit the pipe clamp tail stop into the cutout. Then tighten the clamp so that the handle-end jaw is pressing against the opposite edge of the workpiece.

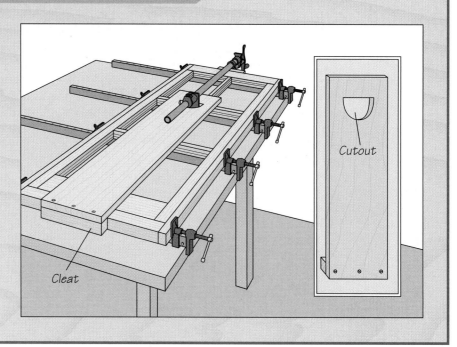

Cleat

Cutout

GLUING UP CARCASES

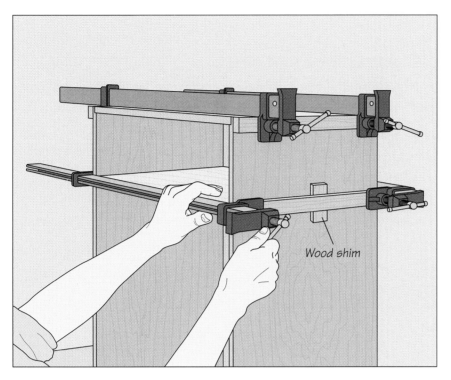

Wood shim

Clamping a carcase with a fixed shelf
Most large carcases can be glued up with bar clamps. After applying adhesive to all the contacting surfaces of the four panels and the shelf, assemble the carcase and install two clamps across the top and bottom panels, protecting the side panels and distributing the pressure with wood pads that extend the full width of the panel. Install a bar clamp across the front and rear of each shelf, again using pads to protect the side panels. Place a ¼-inch-thick wood shim under the center of each pad to focus some of the clamping pressure midway between the edges of the shelving. Tighten the clamps a little at a time *(left)* until glue just begins to squeeze out of the joints.

Gluing up a drawer
Trigger clamps and quick-action bar clamps can be less cumbersome than bar clamps for gluing up drawers and other small carcases. Spread some glue on the contacting surfaces of the joints, then assemble the drawer and set it on a work surface. Install two trigger clamps across the top of the drawer, aligning the bars of the clamps with the front and back of the drawer. Install two quick-action bar clamps across the drawer sides *(right)*, placing a wood pad between the stock and the clamp jaws to avoid marring the wood. Tighten the clamps just enough to fully close the joints, then finish tightening each clamp in turn until a thin glue bead squeezes out of the joints.

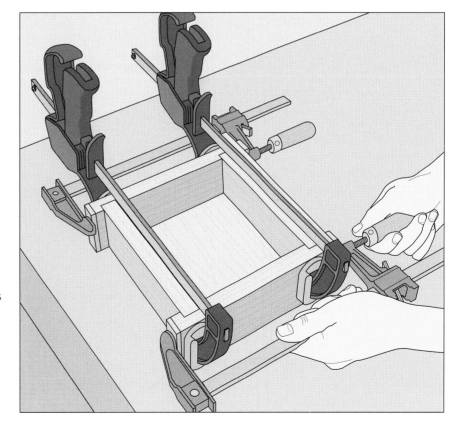

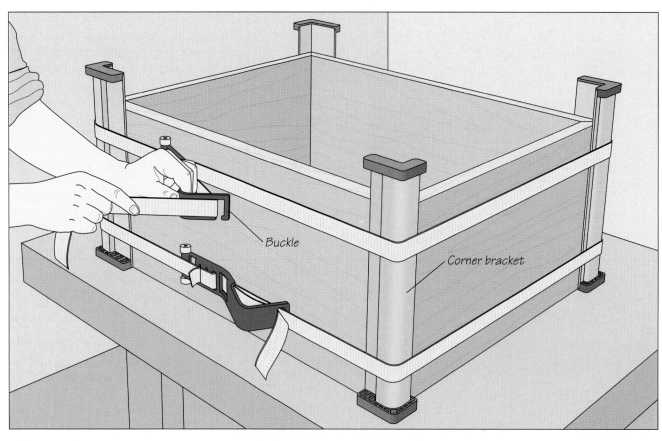

Buckle

Corner bracket

Using a web clamp

A web clamp with corner brackets is especially handy for gluing up carcases with beveled corners. The webs distribute pressure evenly among all four corners, while the brackets help to spread pressure along the length of each joint. To use the type of web clamp set shown here, apply glue to the contacting surfaces of the joints and set the carcase on its back on a work surface. Then fit the corner brackets in place. Wrap the straps around the carcase and tighten them with the buckles before locking them in place (above).

SHOP TIP

Squaring a carcase

Whether you are gluing up a large unit or a small drawer, always check a carcase for square by measuring both diagonals immediately after tightening the clamps. The two results should be identical. If they are not, clamp pressure has pulled the carcase out of square. To remedy the problem, loosen the clamps and slide one jaw of each clamp away from the joint at opposite corners. Tighten the clamps and check again. It may be necessary to repeat the process several times before the parts align properly.

SHOP TIP

Clamping long joints
A gently curving wood pad will ensure that even pressure is applied along the length of a joint. This is critical when bar clamps can only be installed at the ends of the joint, as when gluing a bookcase. To make the pad, cut a gentle curve—no more than ¼ inch deep at its center—from one edge of a 2-inch-wide board the same length as the joint. Set the pad between the panel and the clamp jaws. Tighten the clamps until the pad flattens against the panel.

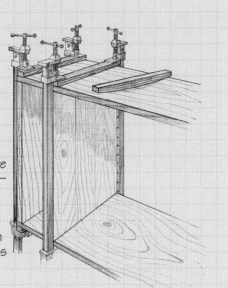

BUILD IT YOURSELF

WEB CLAMPS
You can make your own web clamps out of rope and clamps that you already have in your shop. One device uses two lengths of rope that, when knotted, are slightly shorter than the perimeter of your carcase, and two wood blocks. Bore two holes through each block near the ends, thread one rope through a hole in each block, and knot its ends to the block. Repeat with the other rope, adjusting the length so that the blocks are parallel when set on the carcase. Wrap the ropes and blocks around the carcase, bending cardboard pads around the corners. C clamps pull the blocks toward each other *(left)* and clamp the joints.

A second clamp employs a single handscrew. Wrap a length of rope around the carcase and feed the ends through the clamp. With the tip of the handscrew pressing the rope against the carcase, tighten the back screw to pinch the rope between the back end of the jaws. Holding the handscrew in place, close the front end of the jaws to tighten the rope around the carcase *(above)*.

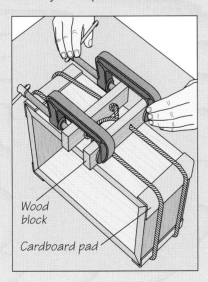

Wood block

Cardboard pad

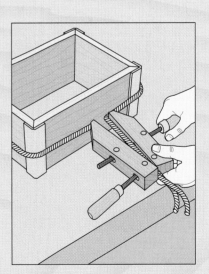

GLUING UP LEGS AND RAILS

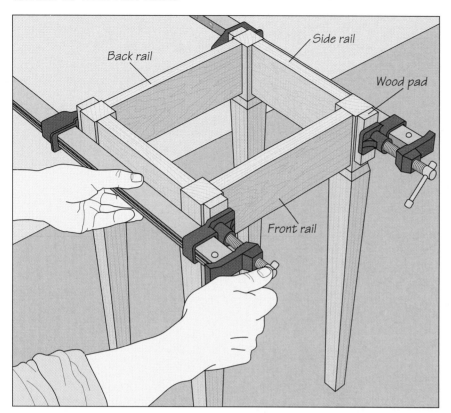

Back rail

Side rail

Wood pad

Front rail

Clamping table legs and rails
Spread glue on the contacting surfaces of the legs and the front and back rails, then fit them together. Protecting the stock with wood pads the same size as the end of the rails, hold the joints together with bar clamps. Carefully straighten the clamps by aligning the bars with the furniture rails, then tighten them until a bead of glue begins to squeeze out of the joints. Once the adhesive has cured, repeat the procedure to fasten the legs to the side rails *(left)*.

Assembling chair legs and rails
Clamp the chair seat face-down to a work surface, and spread glue on all the mating surfaces of the legs and rails. Fit the ends of the rails into the sockets in the legs and wrap the strap of a web clamp around the legs near the bottom of the chair; place corner brackets between the strap and the legs to keep the strap from slipping down the legs. Pull the strap though the buckle until it is snug around the legs. To finish tightening the clamp, turn the ratchet bolt on the buckle with a wrench *(right)*.

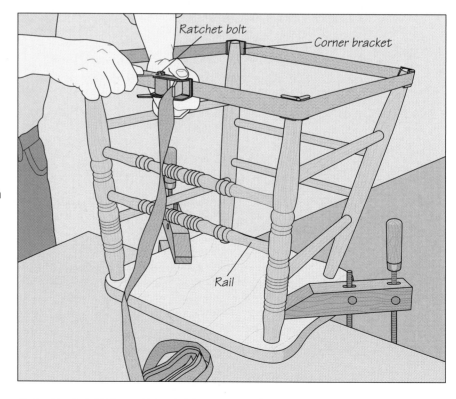

Ratchet bolt

Corner bracket

Rail

GLUING UP MITER JOINTS

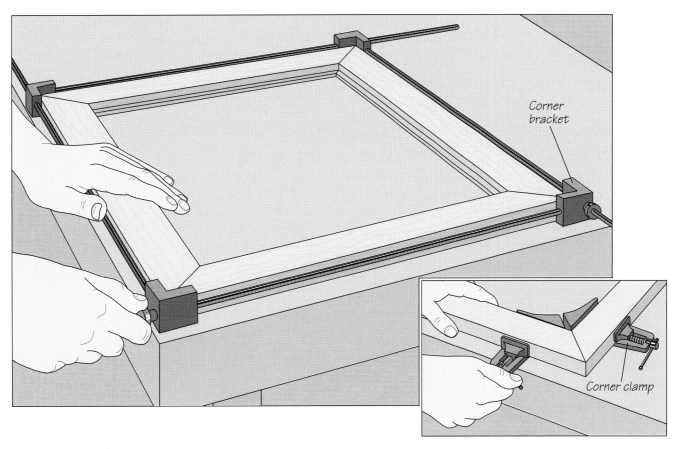

Corner
bracket

Corner clamp

SHOP TIP

An inner tube web clamp
You can fabricate a web clamp for gluing up chair legs with a length of bicycle inner tube and a wood strip. Wrap the inner tube around the legs, making a loop around one leg to prevent slippage. Form another loop midway between two legs. Slip the wood strip through the loop, twist it until the inner tube is tight, and keep the assembly in place with a spring clamp.

Clamping a picture frame
Glue up a picture frame either with a framing clamp or individual corner clamps. With the framing clamp, set the clamp on a work surface with the corner brackets spread as far apart as possible. Apply adhesive on the contacting surfaces of the corner joints and set the picture frame flat inside the clamp. Slide the corner brackets until they all sit flush against the corners of the frame. Tighten the nuts of each bracket a little at a time until all the joints are closed *(above)*. Separate corner clamps are used to secure each corner of the frame *(inset)*. Fit adjoining pieces of the frame in the clamps and, once the four corners are secured, tighten the two screws of each clamp alternately until the joints are tight.

BUILD IT YOURSELF

FRAMING CLAMP

The framing clamp shown at right works as well as a commercial model, but can easily be built in the shop. The dimensions suggested in the illustration will yield a clamp accommodating picture frames measuring up to 24 inches across on a side.

Cut the arms and center blocks from 1-by-3 stock and the corner blocks from ¾-inch plywood. Drill a series of holes for ¼-inch-diameter machine bolts down the middle of the arms; begin 1 inch from one end and space the holes at 1-inch intervals, counterboring the underside to house the bolt heads. Also bore holes through the center blocks about 1 inch from each end. Finally, prepare the corner blocks by drilling two holes through each block: the first for a machine bolt about 1 inch from one end, and a smaller hole about 1½ inches from the same end. Finish by cutting a 90° wedge out of the opposite end, locating the apex of the angle at the center of the second hole drilled.

To assemble the clamp, secure one center block to each pair of arms with bolts, washers, and wing nuts; leave the nuts loose enough to allow the arms to pivot.

To use the clamp, set it on a work surface. Fasten the corner blocks to the arms so that the corners of the frame you are gluing up will sit in them snugly with the center blocks parallel to each other and about ½ inch apart. Use a handscrew to pull the center blocks toward each other, tightening the clamp until all the corner joints are closed *(right, below)*.

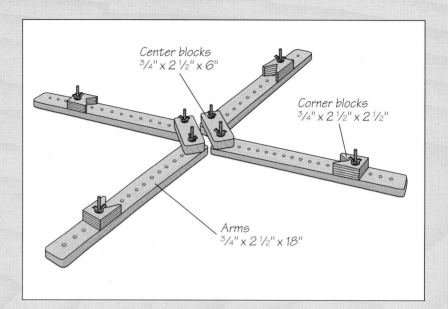

Center blocks
¾" x 2 ½" x 6"

Corner blocks
¾" x 2 ½" x 2 ½"

Arms
¾" x 2 ½" x 18"

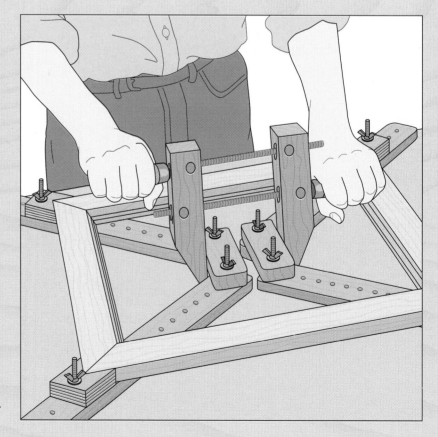

SECURING WORK

Clamps have many uses besides holding work for gluing. During most operations—whether you are boring a hole through a table rail or chopping a mortise in a leg—you will need to clamp your stock to a work surface. Used this way, clamps become "third hands"—or fourth or fifth hands—that allow you to work safely and accurately.

Securing a small or irregularly shaped workpiece to the table of a drill press before boring into it will prevent the drill bit from grabbing the stock and spinning it uncontrollably. Clamping stock to a work surface before cutting it with a circular saw will decrease the risk of kickback. Using clamps to hold edge guides enhances the accuracy of your work, as shown in the photo at right.

The type and arrangement of clamps you use to secure work depend on the dimensions of the stock and the nature of the operation. C clamps are ideal for keeping stock flat *(page 139)*. To hold workpieces like panels and doors upright, C clamps and handscrews work well in combination. Use a pipe or bar clamp in tandem with a shop-made jig and a bench vise to hold a chair or table leg for shaping and finishing *(page 138)*. Whatever the procedure, use as many clamps as necessary to keep a workpiece from wobbling as you work on it. To keep clamps from marring your stock, always place protective pads between the clamp jaws and the wood.

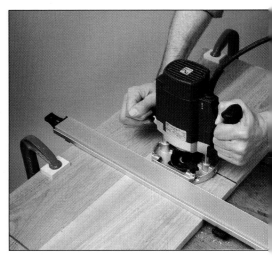

A combination bar clamp and edge guide helps a router cut a dado that is perpendicular to the panel edges.

STEADYING WORKPIECES

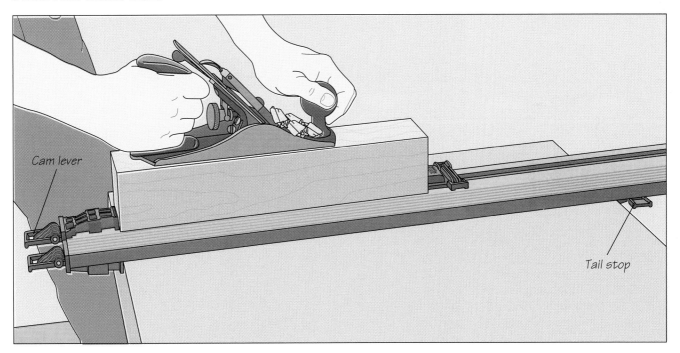

Cam lever

Tail stop

Using a back-to-back clamp
To secure a workpiece without obstructing the top surface of the stock, use a back-to-back clamp. The clamp's low profile keeps it out of the way for operations like planing, as shown. First secure the device to the work surface by butting the fixed head under the clamp against one edge of the table and hooking the tail stop against the table's other edge. Push up the cam lever located directly above the fixed head to secure the clamp. Fasten the workpiece in the clamp by butting one end of your stock against the fixed head on the top of the clamp and sliding the tail stop against the other end. Then push up the second cam lever to lock the device.

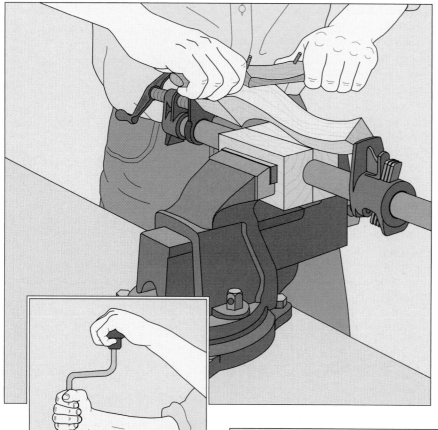

Keeping a workpiece level

To secure a workpiece like the leg shown at left without the risk of marring its contours, use a pipe clamp, a vise, and shop-made support blocks for the clamp. Make the blocks out of two 6-inch-long 2-by-4s. Clamp the blocks together in a handscrew, then set them end down on a backup board atop a work surface. Secure the handscrew and bore a hole into the end grain of the blocks, centering the bit between them *(inset)*; the bit diameter should be slightly smaller than that of the pipe clamp. Saw 1 inch off the edge of the blocks, so that there is about ½ inch of wood above the hole. Fit the blocks around the clamp, secure the assembly in the vise, and fit the workpiece in the clamp.

Backup board

Support block

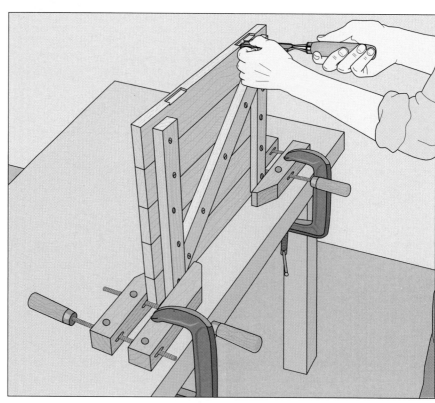

Clamping a door upright

To hold a door or other flat workpiece upright so that you can work on the edge at a comfortable height, use handscrews in tandem with C clamps. Secure the workpiece near its bottom edge in the handscrews, then clamp the handscrews onto the work surface.

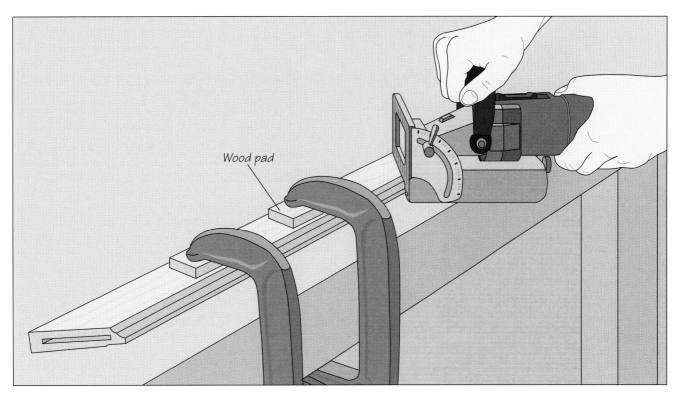

Wood pad

Steadying stock on a work surface

To prevent a workpiece from moving while you cut or drill it, secure it to a work surface. As in the example shown—cutting slots into the end grain of a board with a plate joiner—you will be able to keep both hands on the tool. Set the workpiece on the table, then use C clamps to hold it in position; protect the stock with wood pads. Do not try to make do with just one clamp: The workpiece will have a tendency to pivot when the plate joiner is pushed against the board to make its cut.

SHOP TIP

Holding large panels edge up
For some operations, it may be most convenient to secure a panel upright on edge. For a panel that is too unwieldy to be set on a work table with handscrews and C clamps, use two pipe clamps set on the shop floor. Align the jaws, but face the clamps in opposite directions. The wide stance of the extended pipes should support most workpieces adequately.

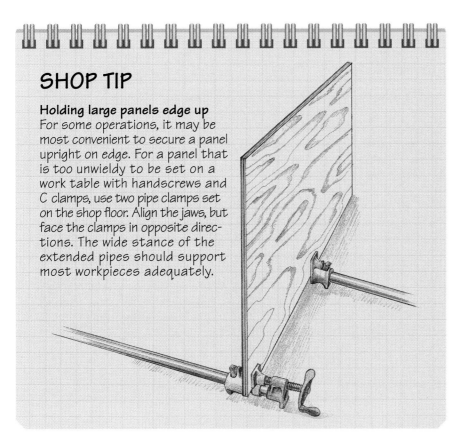

GLOSSARY

A-B-C

Bastard file: A file with relatively deep and widely spaced teeth, providing a coarser cut than second- or smooth-grade files.

Bearing angle: The angle at which a file is held in sharpening the teeth of a handsaw.

Bench stop: A jig fastened or clamped to a work surface to hold a workpiece steady for crosscutting.

Bevel cut: A cut at an angle from face to face along the length or width of a workpiece. *See miter cut.*

Blade set: The amount that saw teeth are offset alternately to the left and to the right, allowing a blade to cut a kerf slightly wider than its own thickness to prevent binding.

Bolster: The enlarged portion of a chisel blade next to the handle.

Bow: A lumber defect characterized by an end-to-end curve along the face of stock.

Burnisher: A rod-like steel tool used in the sharpening process for scrapers.

Burr: A small ridge formed on the flat face of chisel and plane blades as a result of the honing process.

Cap iron: A metal plate screwed to a plane blade, providing a chip breaker and preventing chatter.

Carcase: The box-like frame of a piece of furniture, such as a chest, cabinet, or bookcase.

Chamfer: A bevel cut along the edge of a workpiece.

Cheek: The face of the projecting tenon in a mortise-and-tenon joint.

Chuck: Adjustable jaws that hold drill bits, drivers, and other accessories in a brace or hand drill.

Clamping capacity: The widest span of a clamp's jaws.

Clearance hole: A hole bored in a workpiece to accommodate the shank of a screw.

Compound cut: A saw cut through a workpiece with the blade presented at angles other than 90° relative to the face and edge of the stock.

Concave: A rounded inward shape, like the inside of a bowl.

Contour cut: A cut made along a curved line, usually with a bowsaw or a coping saw.

Convex: A rounded outward shape, like the outside of a bowl.

Counterbore: To drill a hole that permits the head of a screw to sit deep enough below a wood surface to be concealed by a wood plug.

Countersink: Drilling a hole that allows a screw head to lie flush with or slightly below the surface.

Crosscut: A saw cut across the grain of a workpiece.

Cutting gauge: A marking tool featuring a handle, a fence, and a sharp cutting edge for scribing a line on a workpiece.

D-E-F

Dado: A rectangular channel cut into a workpiece.

Dovetail joinery: A method of joining wood at corners by means of interlocking pins and tails; the name derives from the distinctive shape cut into the ends of the joining boards.

Edge gluing: Bonding several boards together edge-to-edge to form a solid panel.

End grain: The arrangement and direction of the wood fibers running across the width of a workpiece when viewed from the ends.

Face gluing: Similar to edge gluing, except that the boards are joined together face-to-face to form a thicker workpiece.

Fence: An adjustable guide to keep the edge of a workpiece a set distance from the cutting edge of a tool.

Firmer chisel: A heavy-duty chisel usually featuring a rectangular blade, typically used with a mallet to cut away large amounts of waste wood.

Frame saw: Any saw with interchangeable blades held taut in a frame; includes the bowsaw, coping saw, and fret saw.

Frog: The surface of a hand plane that supports the blade; in some models, the frog can be moved back and forth to adjust the mouth opening.

G-H-I-J-K-L

Grain: The arrangement and direction of the fibers of wood.

Grit: The density and size of abrasive particles on a piece of sandpaper.

Hogging: A planing operation that removes large quantities of stock quickly.

Honing: The process of converting a rough-ground edge to a smooth, uniform cutting edge.

Hook: A uniform burr turned on the cutting edges of a hand scraper.

Inlay: A decorative strip of metal, wood, or marquetry that is glued in a groove cut into a workpiece.

Jointing: Filing the teeth of a handsaw to the same height; jointing is the first step in sharpening saw teeth. Also, straightening the edge of a workpiece with a jointing plane.

Kerf: A cut made in wood by the width of a saw blade.

Lapping: Rubbing the face of a plane or chisel blade across a sharpening stone to remove the burr that results from honing the blade.

M-N-O
Microbevel: A secondary bevel honed on the front part of the cutting edge of a plane or chisel blade.

Miter cut: A cut that angles across the face of a workpiece; *see bevel cut.*

Mortise: A rectangular, round or oval hole cut into a piece of wood.

Mortise-and-tenon: A joint in which a projecting tenon of one board fits into a mortise on another.

Nail set: A cylindrical, steel tool used to drive the head of a nail below the surface of the work so it can be concealed with filler material.

P-Q-R-S
Paring: Slicing thin wood shavings from a surface with a chisel.

Pilot hole: A hole bored into a workpiece to accommodate the threaded part of a screw; usually slightly smaller than the threaded section of a screw. The hole guides the screw and prevents splitting while giving a firm grip to the threads.

Pin board: The board containing the pins of a dovetail joint; mates with tail board.

Points per inch (PPI): *See teeth per inch.*

Rabbet: A step-like cut in the edge or end of a board; usually forms part of a joint.

Radius: The distance from the center of a circle to its outside edge; equal to one half the diameter.

Reach: The greatest distance that a clamp's jaws are able to extend onto a workpiece.

Rip cut: A cut that follows the grain of a workpiece—usually made along its length.

Screw collar: The unthreaded portion of a screw's shank.

Shooting board: A jig for holding the end grain of a workpiece square to the sole of a hand plane.

Shoulder: The flat portion adjacent to the tenon in a mortise-and-tenon joint; in a dovetail joint, the flat sections between the pins and tails.

Snicking: Vertical ridges on the surface of a workpiece resulting from using a hand plane with a nicked or damaged blade.

Spokeshave: A hand tool with an adjustable cutter for shaping curved surfaces.

Spring steel: A type of steel that is both flexible and strong.

Square: Adjoining surfaces that meet at an angle of 90°.

Squeeze out: The excess glue that is forced from a joint when clamping pressure is applied.

Starting hole: A small hole drilled into the surface of a workpiece to facilitate drilling with a brace or hand drill bit.

Stopped groove: A groove that does not run the full length or width of a workpiece.

Stopped rabbet: A rabbet that does not run the full length or width of the workpiece.

T-U-V-W-X-Y-Z
Tail board: In a dovetail joint, the board containing the tails; mates with pin board.

Tail stop: The movable jaw of a bar or pipe clamp.

Tang: The pointed end of a file or rasp; typically inserted in a handle.

Tearout: The tendency of a blade to tear the fibers of the wood it is cutting, leaving ragged edges on the workpiece.

Teeth per inch (TPI): The number of saw teeth per inch; a measure of a blade's fineness or coarseness in which the lower number indicates a blade that will cut rapidly but roughly. *Points per inch* is a related measure, always one number less than teeth per inch.

Tenon: A protrusion from the end of a board that fits into a mortise.

Tongue: In a tongue-and-groove joint, a protrusion from the edge or end of one board that fits into the groove of another.

INDEX

ACKNOWLEDGMENTS

The editors wish to thank the following:

MEASURING AND MARKING TOOLS
Adjustable Clamp Co., Chicago, IL; Delta International Machinery, Guelph, Ont.;
General Tools Manufacturing Co., Inc., New York, NY; Lee Valley Tools Ltd.,
Ottawa, Ont.; Robert Larson Company, Inc., San Francisco, CA; Stanley Tools,
Division of the Stanley Works, New Britain, CT; Wedge Innovations, San Jose, CA

HANDSAWS
Adjustable Clamp Co., Chicago, IL; American Tool Cos., Lincoln, NE; General
Tools Manufacturing Co., Inc., New York, NY; Hempe Manufacturing Co., Inc.,
New Berlin, WI; Lee Valley Tools Ltd., Ottawa, Ont.; Sandvik Saws and Tools Co.,
Scranton, PA; Stanley Tools, Division of the Stanley Works, New Britain, CT;
Veritas Tools Inc., Ottawa, Ont./Ogdensburg, NY; Vermont American Corp.,
Lincolnton, NC and Louisville, KY

CHISELS AND BORING TOOLS
Adjustable Clamp Co., Chicago, IL; American Tool Cos., Lincoln, NE;
General Tools Manufacturing Co., Inc., New York, NY; Great Neck Saw Mfrs. Inc.
(Buck Bros. Division), Millbury, MA; The Irwin Company, Wilmington, OH;
Lee Valley Tools Ltd., Ottawa, Ont.; Robert Sorby Ltd., Sheffield, U.K./Busy Bee
Machine Tools, Concord, Ont.; Stanley Tools, Division of the Stanley Works,
New Britain, CT; Vermont American Corp., Lincolnton, NC and Louisville, KY;
Woodcraft Supply Corp., Parkersburg, WV

SMOOTHING AND SHAPING TOOLS
Adjustable Clamp Co., Chicago, IL; Anglo-American Enterprises Corp., Somerdale, NJ;
Delta International Machinery, Guelph, Ont.; Great Neck Saw Mfrs., Inc., Mineola,
MA; Lee Valley Tools Ltd., Ottawa, Ont.; Record Tools Inc., Pickering, Ont.;
Robert Larson Company, Inc., San Francisco, CA; Veritas Tools Inc., Ottawa,
Ont./Ogdensburg, NY; Vermont American Corp., Lincolnton, NC and Louisville, KY

STRIKING AND FASTENING TOOLS
Adjustable Clamp Co., Chicago, IL; Delta International Machinery, Guelph, Ont.;
Great Neck Saw Mfrs. Inc. (Buck Bros. Division), Millbury, MA; Stanley Tools,
Division of the Stanley Works, New Britain, CT; Vermont American Corp.,
Lincolnton, NC and Louisville, KY

CLAMPS
Adjustable Clamp Co., Chicago, IL; Advanced Machinery Imports Ltd.,
New Castle, DE; American Tool Cos., Lincoln, NE; Griset Industries, Inc.,
Santa Ana, CA; Hitachi Power Tools U.S.A. Ltd.; Record Tools Inc., Pickering, Ont.;
Steiner-Lamello A.G. Switzerland/Colonial Saw, Kingston, MA;
Vermont American Corp., Lincolnton, NC and Louisville, KY

The following persons also assisted in the preparation of this book:

Donna Curtis, Lorraine Doré, Graphor Consultation, Leonard Lee

PICTURE CREDITS

Cover Robert Chartier
6, 7 Mark Tucker
8, 9 Raymond Gendreau
10, 11 Ian Gittler